6  16  22  28

## AUGUST 2023

# CONTENTS

## FEATURES

**5**    Editorial

**80**    **Q&A** Professor Jezdimir Knezevic

**88**    **The Stand** with Advergus Taylor

**90**    **Skills In Demand**

**93**    **Breaking the Barriers in Reliability Report**
Reliability Leadership Foundation:
People and Culture at Work Consortium

## ARTICLES

**6**    **The Introduction of the S-D-I-P-F Safety Reliability Curve**
Terrence O'Hanlon

**16**    **Plan-Do-Check-Act: The Importance of a Continuous Improvement Cycle**
Mike Meen

**22**    **Repair or Replace? Some Thoughts**
Ron Moore

**28**    **Critical Thinking in Risk-Based Decisions**
Brian J. Pertuit and Joseph A. DeCuir

**36** Ultrasound for Condition Monitoring and Acoustic Lubrication for Condition-Based Maintenance
Jim Hall

**44** Achieving Trouble Free Bearing Life Through Defect Elimination
Phil Hendrix

**50** Bridging the Proactive Maintenance Knowledge GAP: Overcoming the Dunning-Kruger Effect
John Crossan

**56** 13 Project Management Fundamentals to Support Successful CMMS-EAM Optimization Projects
Jason Weis

**68** 7 Steps to Criticality Analysis for Capital Projects and Sustainment Planning
Mike Castro

**76** Making a Business Case for Condition-Based Maintenance
Maciej Kuczyński

# uptime

**CEO/PUBLISHER**
Terrence O'Hanlon
terrence@reliabilityweb.com

**EDITOR**
Kirstin Simpson

**TECHNICAL EDITOR**
Dave Reiber

**CONTRIBUTING WRITERS**
Mike Castro, John Crossan, Joseph A. DeCuir, Jim Hall, Phil Hendrix, Jezdimir Knezevic, Maciej Kuczyński, Mike Meen, Ron Moore, Terrence O'Hanlon, Brian J. Pertuit, Jason Weis, Reliability Leadership Foundation, People and Culture at Work Consortium

**ASSOCIATE EDITOR**
Maryellen Cicione

**DESIGNER**
Jocelyn Brown

**SALES & ADVERTISING**
Maura Abad
Global Relationship Leader
crm@reliabilityweb.com

**EDITORIAL INFORMATION**
Please address submissions of case studies, procedures, practical tips and other correspondence to Terrence O'Hanlon
terrence@reliabilityweb.com

**ARTICLE SUBMISSIONS**
publishing@reliabilityweb.com

**SUBSCRIPTIONS**
To purchase *Uptime*® Bookazine visit www.ReliabilityMarketplace.com

**POSTMASTER**
**Send Address Changes To:**
Reliabilityweb.com
ATTN: *Uptime* Bookazine
PO Box 425, Blair, NE 68008

**Copyright© 2023, Reliabilityweb.com. All rights reserved.**

ISBN: 979-8-9884121-2-0

No part of *Uptime*® bookazine may be reproduced or transmitted in any form or by any means without the prior express written consent of Reliabilityweb.com. In the U.S., *Uptime*® is a registered trademark of Reliabilityweb.com.

*Uptime*® bookazine is published quarterly by
Reliabilityweb.com • PO Box 425 • Blair, Nebraska • 68008 • 888-575-1245.
*Uptime*® bookazine is an independently produced publication of Reliabilityweb.com.
The opinions expressed herein are not necessarily those of Reliabilityweb.com.

Reliabilityweb.com®, Uptime®, RELIABILITY®, A Culture of Reliability®, Certified Reliability Leader®, Reliability Leadership®, Reliability Leadership Institute®, The Reliability Conference™, Reliability for Everyone™, Reliability Framework™, Reliability Leader™ and Reliability Partners™ are registered trademarks or trademarks of Reliabilityweb.com. in the USA and several other countries.

# Editorial

**Dear Esteemed Readers of *Uptime*® bookazine,**

We're overjoyed to unveil the transformative relaunch of *Uptime*® magazine as *Uptime*® bookazine. This is a significant milestone on our journey toward forging the future of the industry. As we step into this new era, be assured that our cornerstone remains the same: dedication to exceptional content and invaluable industry insights.

Our rejuvenated publication marries the invaluable wisdom of the past with the trailblazing vision of the future. In its fresh avatar, *Uptime* promises to remain your trusted companion, showcasing an exemplary blend of high-caliber articles and expert thought leadership. Its avant-garde solutions underscore our standing as the first port of call for professionals in industrial maintenance, asset management, and reliability engineering.

*Uptime* bookazine pledges to be your trusted companion. It strives to empower you to make a difference, foster innovation, and push boundaries. Within these pages, you will find actionable insights that catalyze your career and propel your operations to the pinnacle of success.

Our content includes cutting-edge technologies, best practices, enlightening case studies, and the pulse of industry trends. We continue to focus on enabling safer, sustainable, reliable, and thriving workplaces.

We invite you to join us on this extraordinary odyssey of evolution. Together, we'll script the future narrative of industrial maintenance, reliability, and asset management. Prepare yourselves for a journey. Explore pages teeming with inspiration, information, and the intellectual arsenal you need to scale unprecedented heights of success!

Warmly from the heart of *Uptime*,

*Terrence O'Hanlon*
Terrence O'Hanlon
CEO and Publisher

> "This is a significant milestone on our journey toward forging the future of the industry."

# THE INTRODUCTION OF THE S-D-I-P-F SAFETY RELIABILITY CURVE

Terrence O'Hanlon

## The S-D-I-P-F Safety Reliability Curve Begins With the 1979 Birth of the P to F Interval

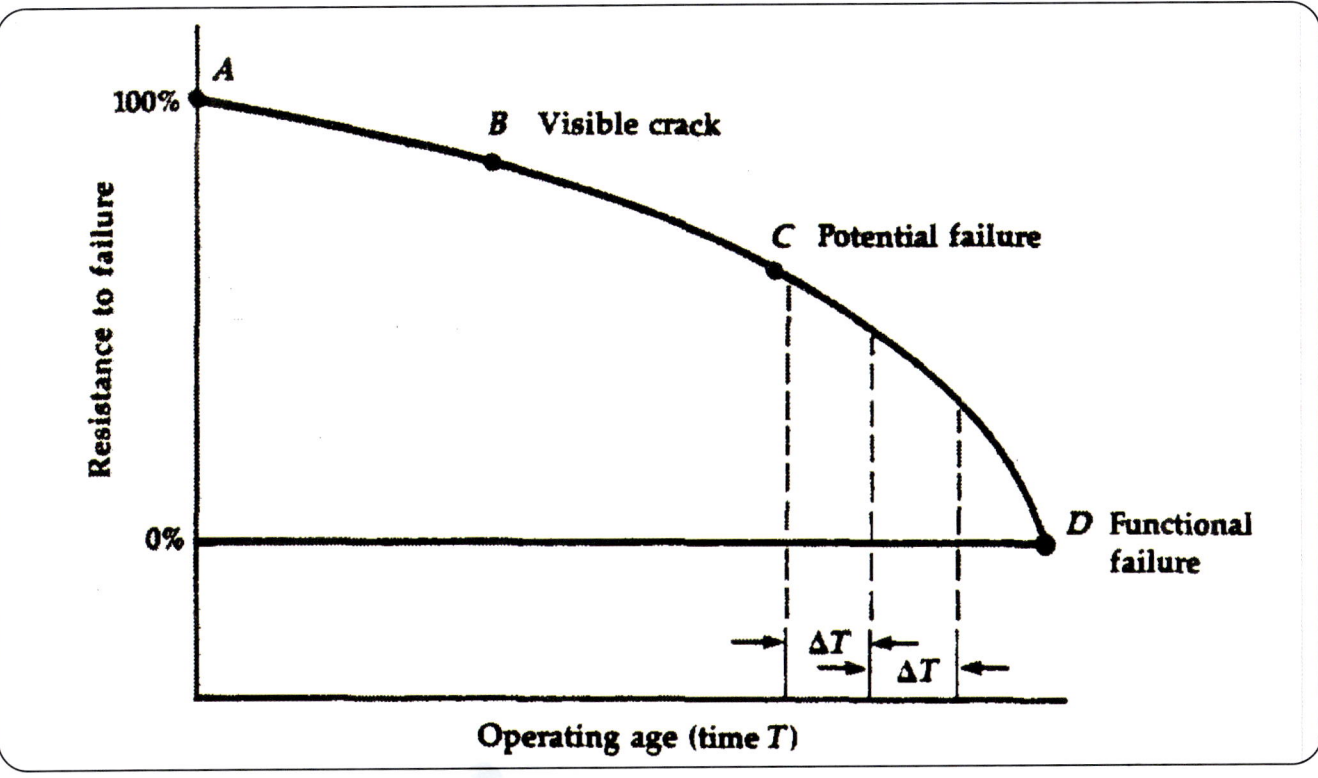

**Figure 1:** Original P to F curve (Reliability-Centered Maintenance report by Nowlan and Heap)

*"Determining the interval for on-condition inspection of an item subject to metal fatigue. Once the rate of decline in failure resistance has been determined, an inspection interval "ΔT" is established that provides ample opportunity to detect a potential [P] failure before a functional [F] failure can occur."*

Excerpt from: F.S. Nowlan, "Reliability-Centered Maintenance," 1979

Over 40 years later, many of the benefits from Stanley Nowlan's and Howard Heap's *Reliability-Centered Maintenance* report are still setting the standard for achieving asset reliability.

Setting inspection periodicities based on failure mechanisms and failure modes is a basic maintenance building block for high reliability organizations. The approach described in the P-F curve is proven and forms the center of what many refer to as predictive maintenance, however, the Uptime® Elements A Reliability Framework and Asset Management System™ refers to it as asset condition management (ACM). The basic concept is to use sensors to detect a defect prior to it causing a functional failure. The repair or renewal can be scheduled prior to more severe damage and we have a longer scheduling envelope to avoid interrupting production or operations.

As solid as the original P to F curve is, it is applied in the final stages of an asset's lifecycle and does not attempt a whole life asset view.

Various stakeholders, who can obtain or remove value from assets at various stages of their life and their roles in the organization, typically work

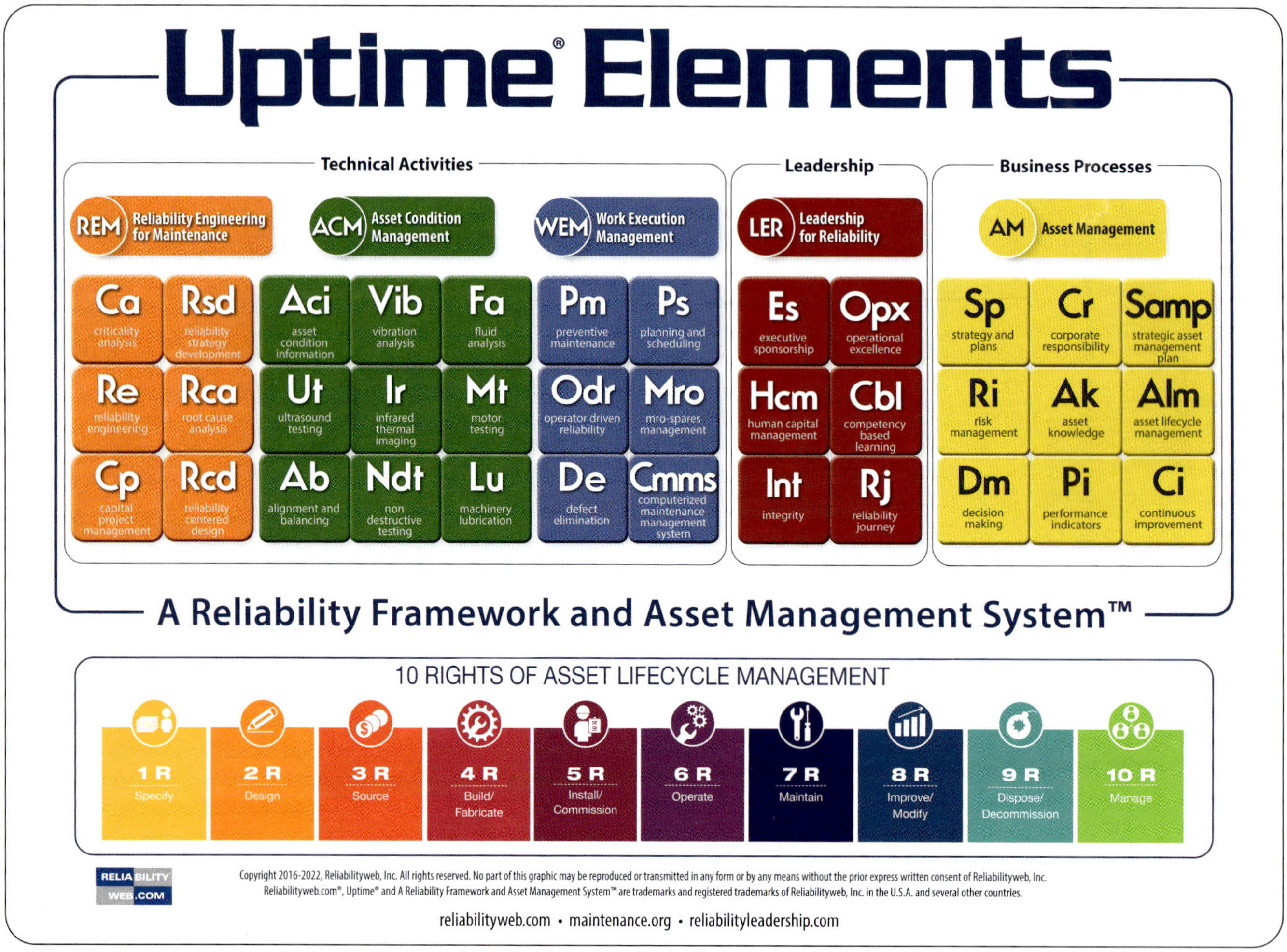

**Figure 2:** The Uptime® Elements A Reliability Framework and Asset Management System (Terrence O'Hanlon, Reliabilityweb.com)

in silos. A critical success factor for assuring value from assets is to better understand the dynamic connections between reliability strategy development and asset criticality and risk management and decision-making and asset condition management and preventive maintenance and work execution management and asset knowledge and asset management across the assets' lifecycles and based in policy, strategy and plan to align intentional thought, effective action and efficient effort toward creating value from assets aligned toward achievement of organizational objectives.

That alignment and energy must be intentional for a group to achieve a new future that was not going to happen anyway.

Asset management, as described by the Uptime® Elements A Reliability Framework and Asset Management System, creates an intentional management system or, more specifically, an asset management system to ensure opportunity and risk are managed or treated at the asset level that is appropriate for achieving organizational objectives as set by top management through value generated by the assets.

## The Time Machine

One of the challenges with reliability is that its effects and causes are disconnected in time. Reliability decisions pay significant dividends, but they are paid slowly, over long periods of

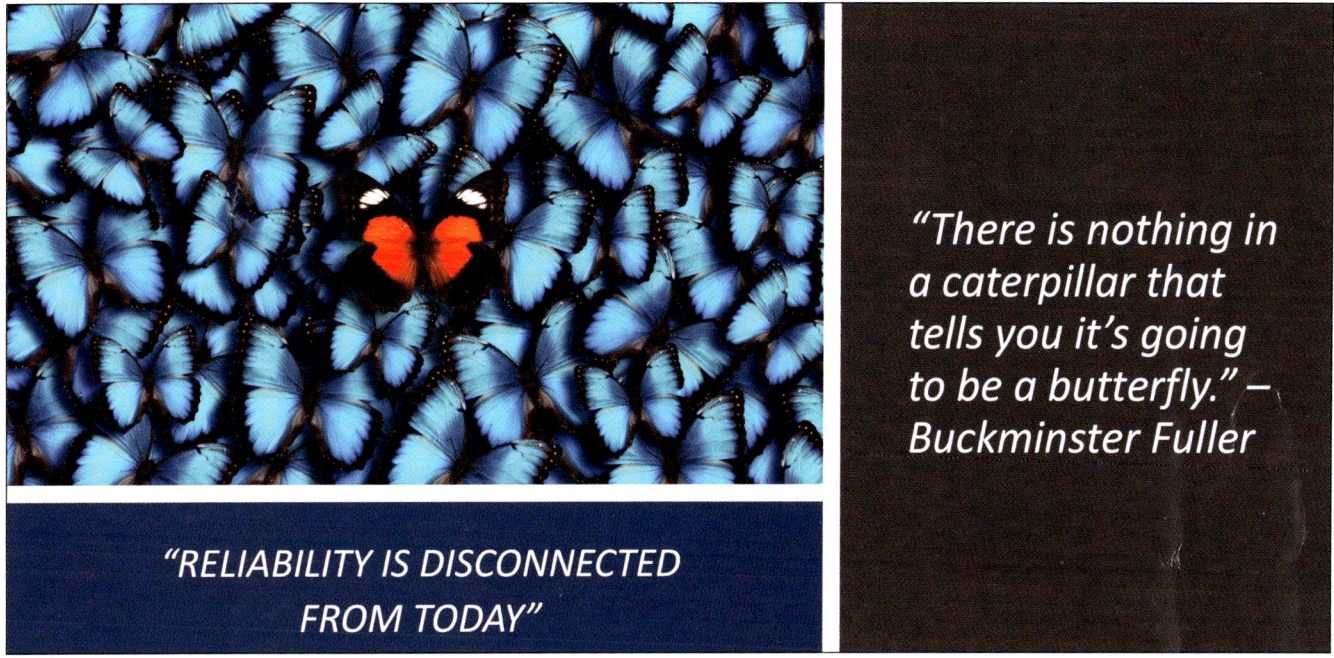

**Figure 3:** There is nothing in a caterpillar that tells you it's going to be a butterfly - Buckminster Fuller (Terrence O'Hanlon, Reliabilityweb.com)

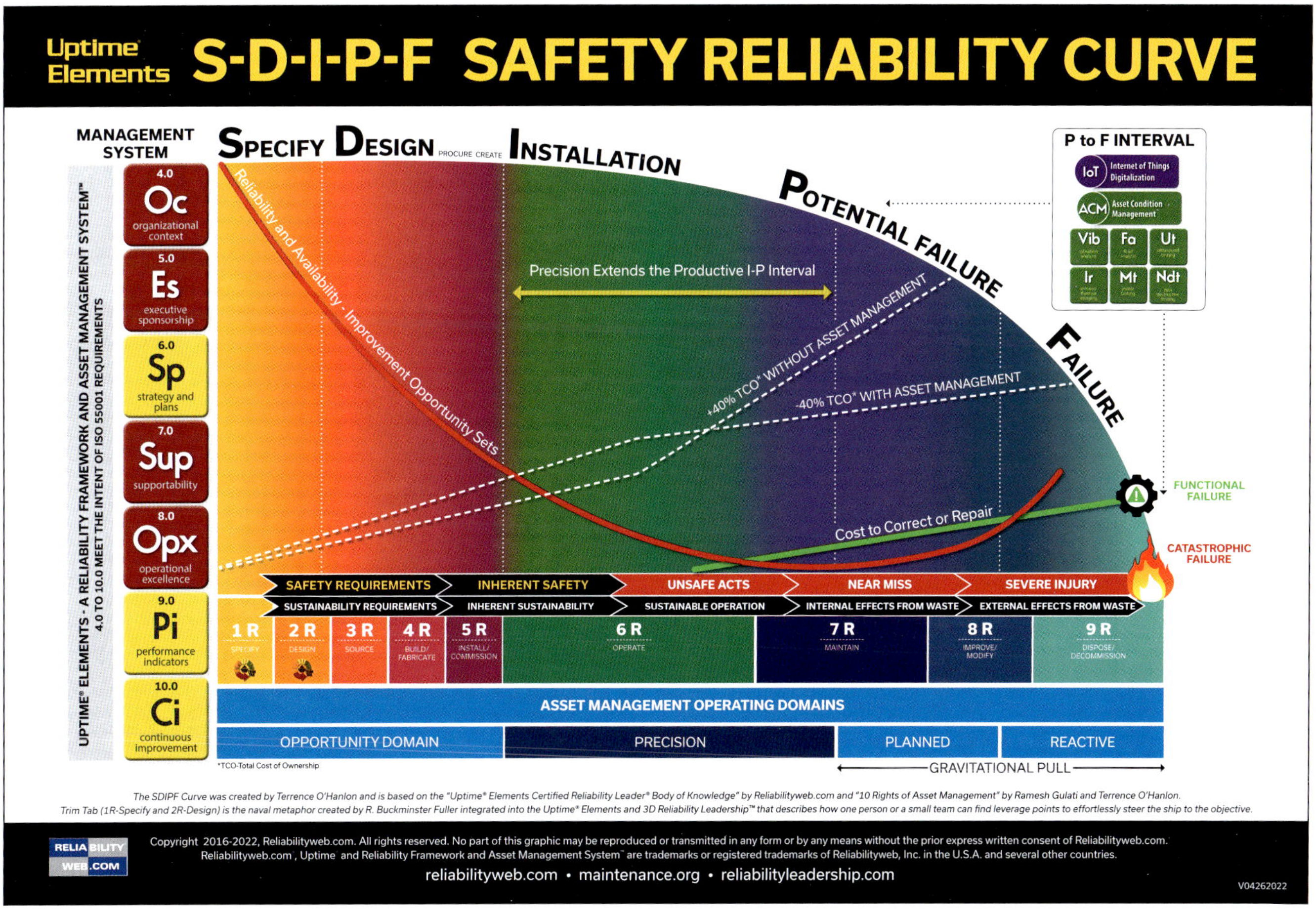

**Figure 4:** The S-D-I-P-F Safety Reliability Curve

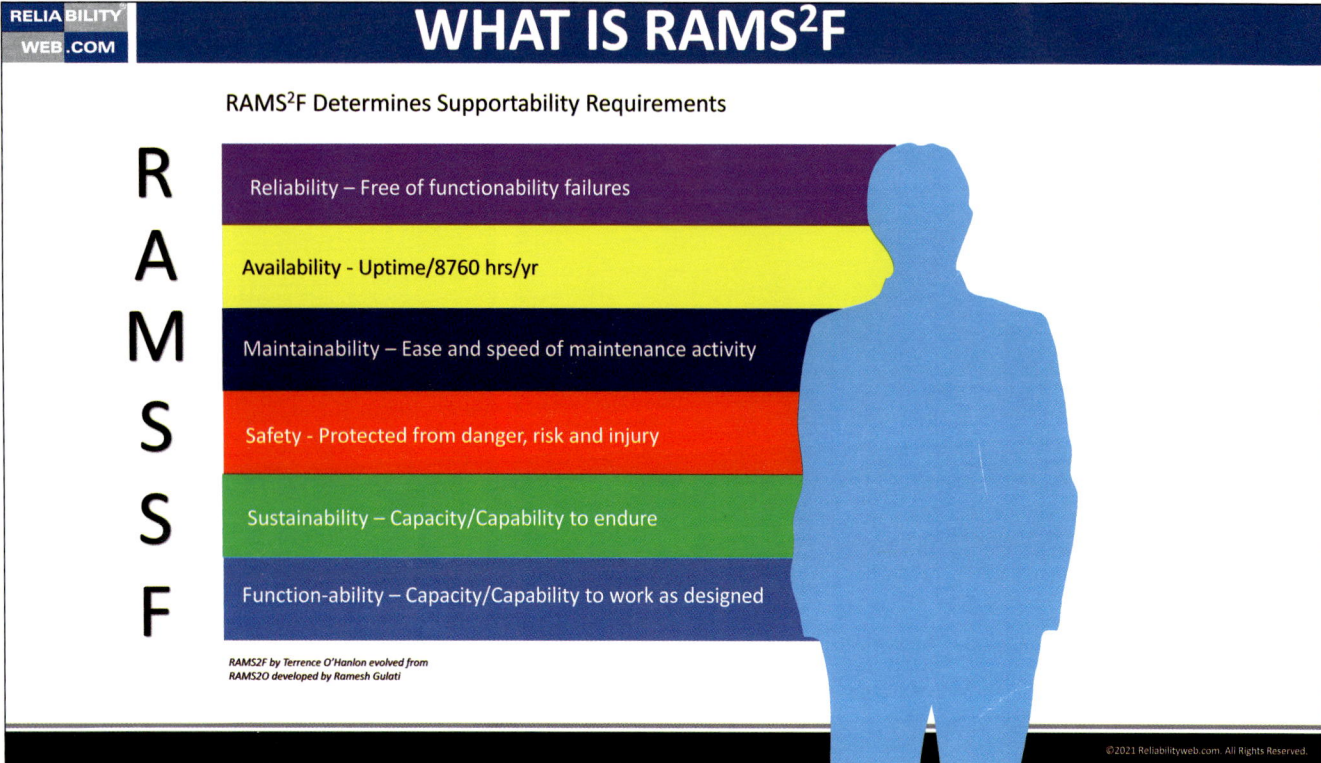

**Figure 5:** What is RAMS²F by Terrence O'Hanlon

time. With management typically focused on short-term projects and goals, it is easy for organizations to depreciate reliability and realize a loss of consistent value generation from assets in a much more rapid fashion than it took to gain it.

The fallacy of improving reliability through maintenance has been chased for the past 40 years and like Sisyphus pushing his rock up the hill, a few dedicated teams of driven people make it to the top through a noble hero's journey, but the rock inevitably rolls back down again within two to three years. The best practice maintenance expert advice sends the team to the *planned domain* where they develop systems to anticipate and deal with failures through efficient maintenance processes. The only problem with this approach is that maintenance cannot influence all the causes of breakdowns. The planned domain is unstable and quickly becomes a *reactive-planned domain*, with an almost unescapable gravitational pull of failures caused by defects beyond the control or influence of the maintenance department to remove them or inspect and monitor to detect them.

The S-D-I-P-F Safety Reliability Curve is a visualization that attempts to graphically "bend time" to amplify the benefit of investing in and applying early reliability and sustainability efforts by showing a lifetime snapshot of the asset over time.

All due respect is given to Stanley Nowlan and Howard Heap, however, their excellent P-F curve work was intended strictly as an on-condition monitoring periodicity determinant. It is with high respect that their work is used in creating the S-D-I-P-F curve.

### Some of the ideas expressed in the S-D-I-P-F curve:

- It visually expresses the full asset lifecycle phases from a *"x for Reliability"* lens.

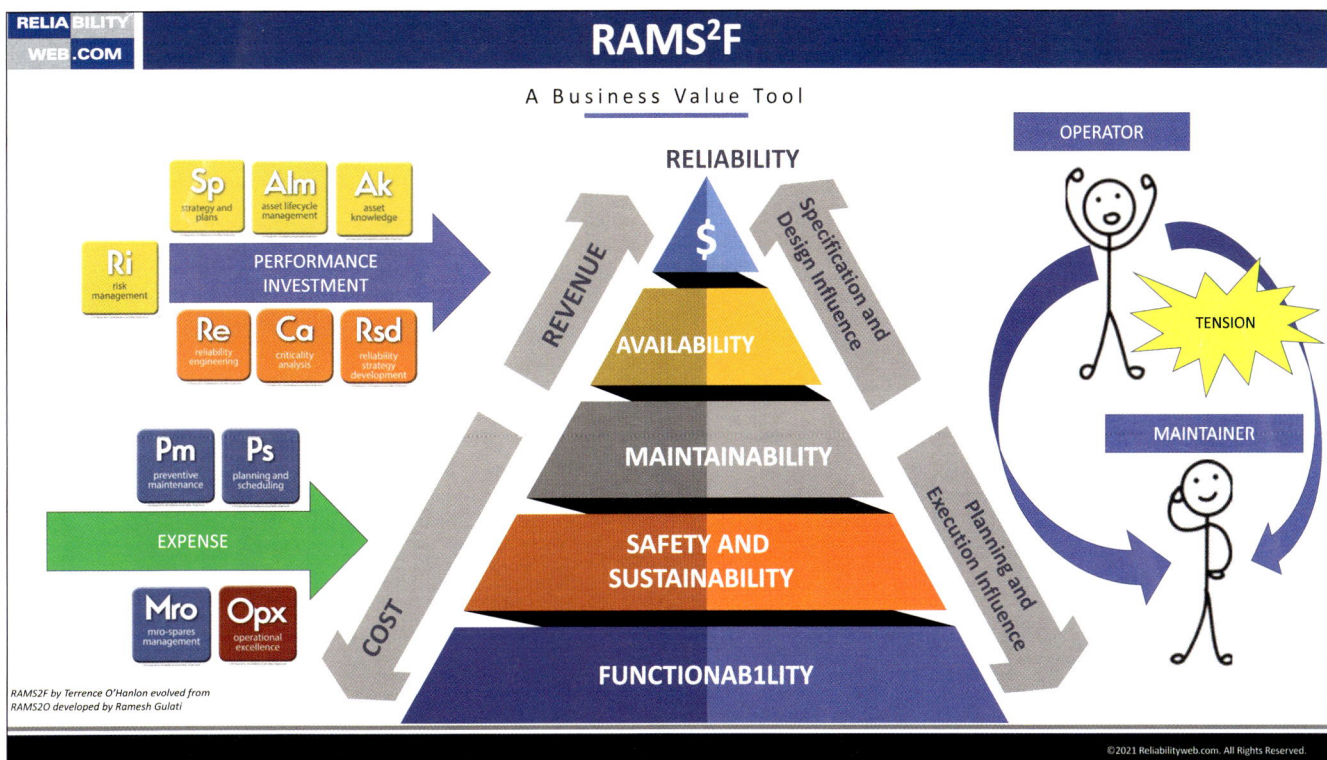

**Figure 6:** RAMS²F by Terrence O'Hanlon

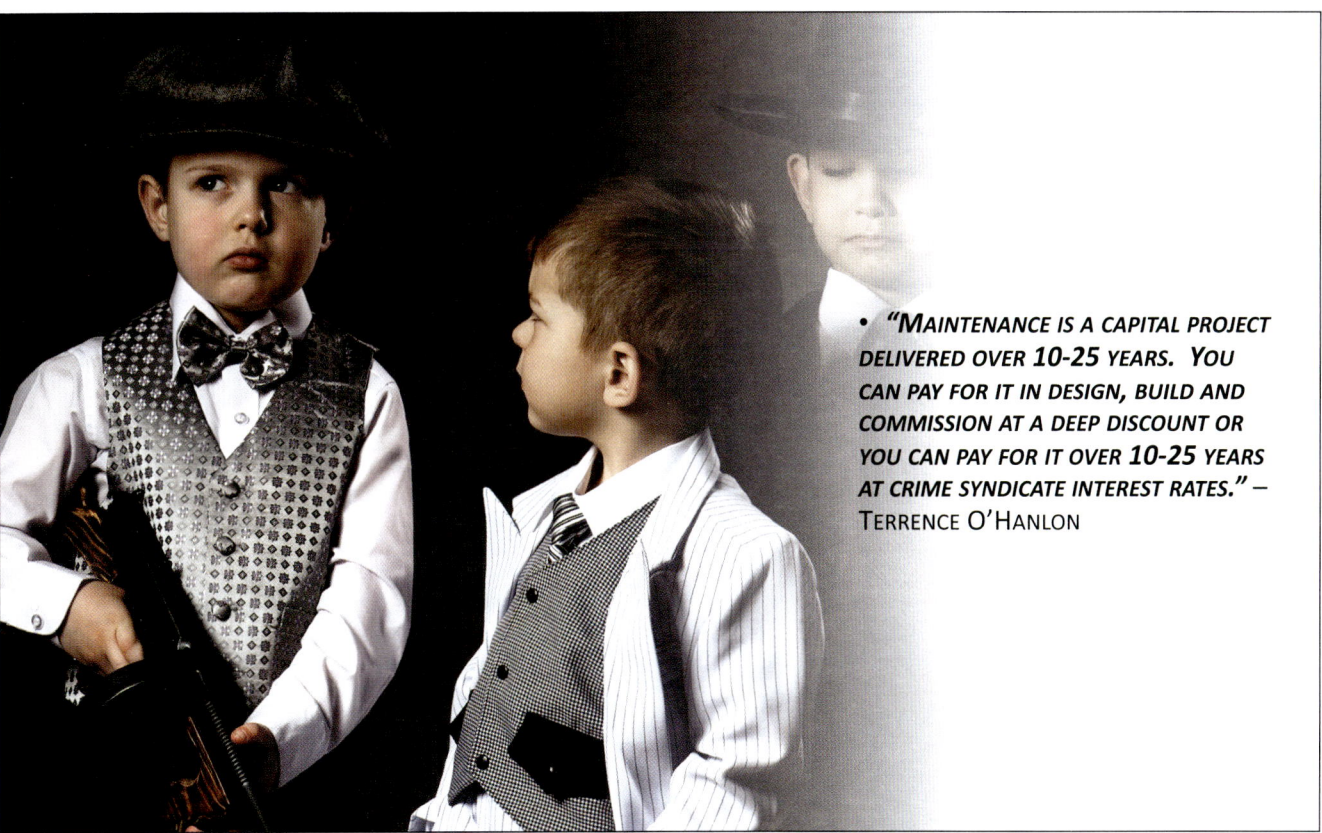

- *"Maintenance is a capital project delivered over 10-25 years. You can pay for it in design, build and commission at a deep discount or you can pay for it over 10-25 years at crime syndicate interest rates."* – Terrence O'Hanlon

**Figure 7:** Maintainability should be considered during design to leverage total cost of ownership

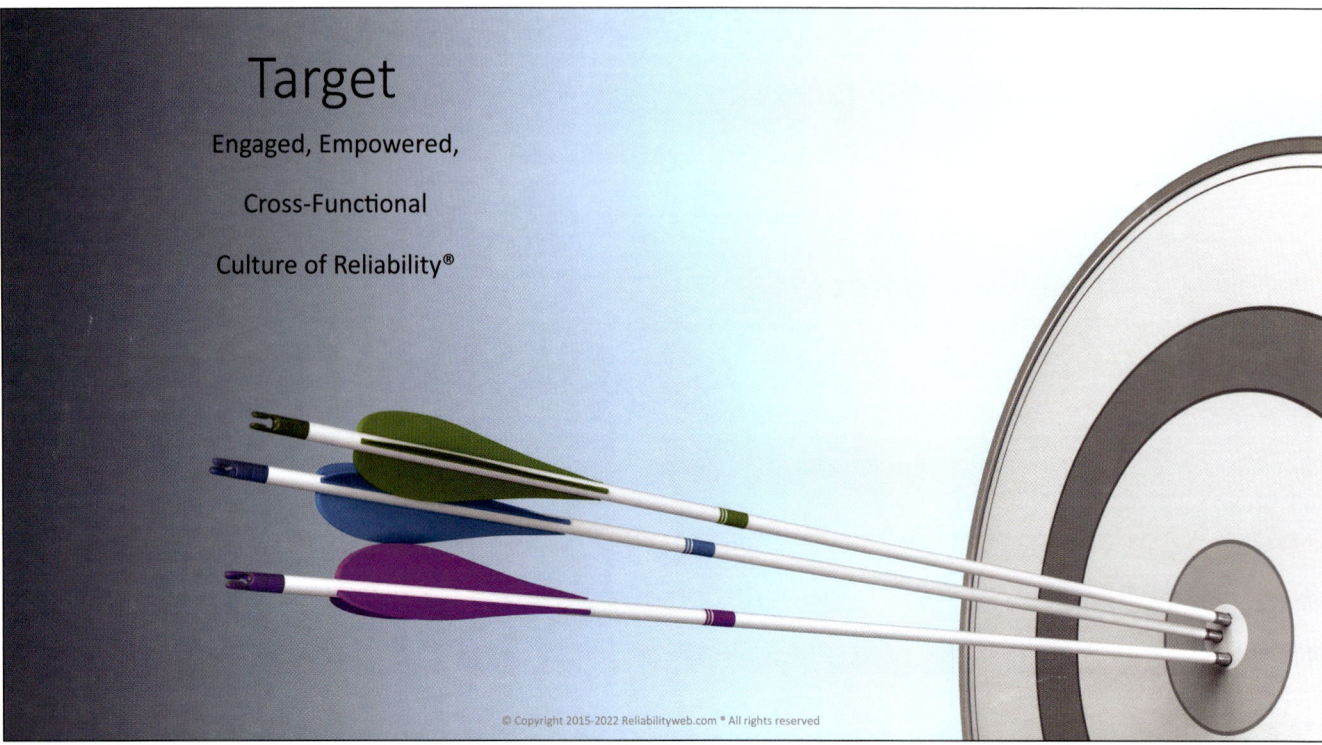

**Figure 8:** The target to achieve is an engaged, empowered, cross-functional culture of reliability

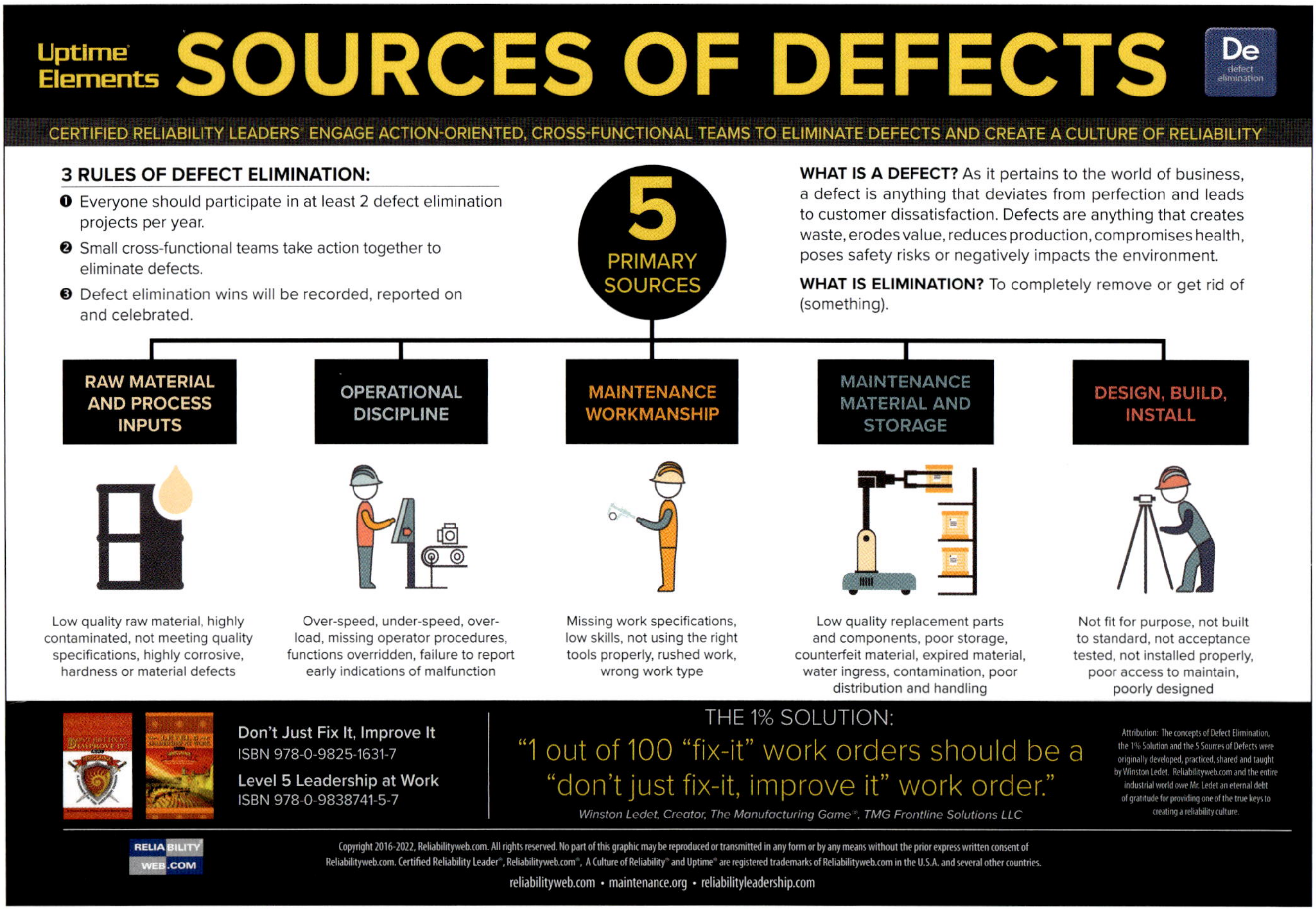

**Figure 9:** Sources of defects

- It visually expresses the *leverage* or *influence level* or *opportunity sets* for improving reliability and availability over the asset's lifecycle phases.
- It visually expresses total cost of ownership with and without formal asset management.
- It visually expresses the greatest opportunity sets for reliability, sustainability and maintainability to improve the asset itself early on in the asset's lifecycle phases.
- It expresses respect for the original intent of the P-F curve as a method to determine asset condition monitoring periodicity.
- It visually expresses operating maturity domains and encourages moving to the precision and expansive domains.
- It visually expresses the gravitational pull (p to f repeating cycle) of the reactive-planned domain, where systems have been put in place to anticipate and plan for asset failures, however, significant unplanned failures continue to surprise the team and consume resources.
- It shows the limited reliability and availability improvement opportunities in the operation and maintenance phases.

**What ideas do you see? Note them here:**

1. _____

2. _____

3. _____

## Some RAMS²F Embedded in S-D-I-P-F Curve

**Some of the more technical aspects of the RAMS²F asset lifecycle theory are embedded in the S-D-I-P-F curve:**

**AVAILABILITY** is defined as the probability that the system is operating properly when it is requested for use.

**RELIABILITY** is the probability that a system or asset will operate in a satisfactory manner for a specified manner for a specified period of time when used under stated conditions.

Both reliability and availability can be specified, predicted and measured. The biggest opportunities to improve them exist during the early asset lifecycle phases of specification, design, procurement, build/create, and install/commission. Once in operation, the opportunity sets to improve the inherent reliability is limited.

**MAINTAINABILITY** is defined as the probability that a failed system will be restored or repaired to a specified condition within a period of time when maintenance is performed in accordance with prescribed procedures.

Maintainability can be specified, predicted and measured. The biggest opportunities to improve it is through planning and execution.

Maintenance includes all scheduled and unscheduled actions necessary for retaining an item or restoring it to an operational condition. Maintenance includes repair, replace, remove, restore, renew, testing, modification, inspection, servicing calibration, overhaul, condition verification, and so on. Maintenance may or may not result in downtime. Maintenance is usually a major contributor to lifecycle cost.

## Some Cultural Aspects Embedded in the S-D-I-P-F Curve

The target to achieve is the expansive opportunity domain through the precision domain by creating an engaged, empowered, cross-functional reliability leadership culture.

Traditionally, the maintenance team owns breakdowns or unreliability. They are the specialists with the know-how to react quickly to get the assets

**Figure 10:** The 10 Rights of Asset Management book was written by Ramesh Gulati and Terrence O'Hanlon

back online. They repair, replace, renew, restore and inspect.

Unfortunately, many organizations also default responsibility for reliability to the maintenance teams without providing all the controlling influences, setting up a cycle of unplanned breakdowns that often lead to a safety, environmental, or economic catastrophe.

Engineering, Procurement, Operations, Quality, HR/HCM, Training, Safety, Stores, Capital Projects, IT, Sales, Marketing and top management are all stakeholders in reliability and make decisions that enable and disable reliability. A coordination effort, guided by policy, strategy and plan, is required to ensure intentional value.

Getting these stakeholders engaged is what the Uptime Elements A Reliability Framework and Asset Management System is all about. The S-D-I-P-F curve is designed to help you tell the story that you need to tell to engage those stakeholders who can enable your reliability journey! Please let the Reliabilityweb.com team know how they can support that.

The S-D-I-P-F curve is created as part of the Uptime Elements A Reliability Framework and Asset Management System by Terrence O'Hanlon. He is open to hearing your ideas around the S-D-I-P-F Safety Reliability Curve.

**Terrence O'Hanlon,** CMRP, and CEO of Reliabilityweb.com® and Publisher of Uptime® bookazine, is an asset management leader, specializing in reliability and operational excellence. He is a popular keynote presenter and the coauthor of the book, *10 Rights of Asset Management: Achieve Reliability, Asset Performance and Operational Excellence.* www.reliabilityweb.com

# Plan-Do-Check-Act:

## The Importance of a Continuous Improvement Cycle

Mike Meen

Many maintenance programs grow organically over the years and end up focusing mainly on breakdown and unplanned maintenance. During my years of managing maintenance and integrity operations, I have seen many technicians work in firefighting mode, typically resulting in preventative planned maintenance taking a hit. To implement an effective and efficient work management system within your organization, you must implement and follow a continuous improvement cycle.

One of the key continuous improvement systems is the Plan-Do-Check-Act (or PDCA) approach. This method, also often referred to as the Demming or Shewhart cycle, encourages continuous improvement through consistent review and implementation of process-based updates.

Once you progress your organization to a high level of maturity in the PDCA cycle, you will find yourself becoming highly efficient in terms of work management processes and delivery of maintenance activities. With a **plan** of activities in place, you can **execute** work methodically, **check** to

**PLAN**     **DO**     **CHECK**     **ACT**

ensure that all work is being carried out effectively and that the plan is being upheld and **act** on the checks by implementing corrective routines and adjusting plans.

## PDCA vs. IPSECA

You may have encountered a similar system to PDCA in the form of **IPSECA**. This is also a continuous improvement cycle:

**Identification:** Used to define what and where work needs to be done.

**Planning and Prioritization:** Determining the cost, task, labor and material requirements for executing the work and communicating the urgency of identified work.

**Scheduling:** The prioritized work scopes over a given time and the sequence of activities, preparing the work space and resources for the work.

**Execution:** The physical execution of the work in accordance with safe work order instructions and in alignment with the agreed schedule.

**Completion:** The feedback of information for updating both recurring planned work and corrective orders to ensure that accurate historical data is captured. Returning the worksite to a safe condition and handing back the site to operations.

**Analysis:** The analysis of the work performed to drive continuous improvement over time.

**Here, you can see how IPSECA falls into the PDCA cycle:**

**PLAN** - Identify, plan and prioritize;

**DO** - Schedule, prepare and execute;

**CHECK** - Complete and analyze;

**ACT** - Correct any defects and systematically remove waste from the process.

## How the PDCA cycle aids effective work management

Effective maintenance identification, planning and scheduling is vital for every asset: Not only does it enable efficient work execution, it also has a direct impact on production and safety targets as well as operational expenditure.

An almost daily challenge faced by maintenance or asset managers, however, is planned maintenance vs. unplanned corrective maintenance. When unplanned work disrupts the frozen plan and weekly schedules and is prioritized over scheduled tasks, you start accumulating a backlog. The biggest challenge is deciding whether this unplanned work should take priority over other work that has already been planned and scheduled.

In this instance, prioritization is essential. When you identify any work, ask yourself: What is the reliability of components based on the risk profile of a piece of equipment? You can identify a risk profile by determining the consequences of the piece of equipment failing and what the probability of that failure is. From there, you can prioritize your workload and manage corrective maintenance more efficiently.

Your review should justify its prioritization above planned maintenance — this unplanned, corrective work should have a high enough priority to allow it to be broken into schedules. However, by applying a structured, risk-based approach, you may often find (when it isn't obvious) that the unplanned work isn't of a higher priority and that your scheduled work is actually of greater importance. In that case, the unplanned work should be challenged and pushed out to the optimum point where practical.

During planned work, you need to maintain the discipline of allocating time and resources in parallel with your asset norms, and then, through proactive management, altering the ratio to favor PM work. By aiming or adhering to this regime, maintenance will get back on track and create headroom towards more proactive rather than reactive interventions.

When executing work, ensure that the site, plant and people are all prepared to complete the work in the plan. Ensuring that tools, resources and consumables are ready to go at the point of use allows for the plan to be efficiently and successfully followed.

> **When executing work, ensure that the site, plant and people are all prepared to complete the work in the plan.**

Regularly checking your maintenance plans against the work being executed and having visibility of data around your plan attainment can be extremely useful, as it allows you to:

- Drill down and understand why you are unable to achieve your plan;
- Unearth problems you did not previously see;
- Open up discussions with your team so that you can work together to fix any issues.

> **Define a metric that suits your business for measuring compliance against your "plan attainment."**

Define a metric that suits your business for measuring compliance against your "plan attainment." Regular reviews of this KPI and contributing factors will encourage investigation and allow for critical conversations to take place. By understanding the reasons for non-compliance, realistic and tangible actions can be put in place to help the maintenance team comply with and adapt to the maintenance plan. The implementation of corrective actions into the work execution plan will then lead you into the Act stage of the PDCA cycle.

Finally, the Act stage is key to the improvement cycle, as the planned, executed and checked work can allow informed changes to be made. When checking and closing work, the priority, above all else, should be that the site is left in a safe and clean condition and the equipment is operating to the highest standard possible. Procedure and process should be checked by making sure that the data is entered into the system, so that when you move on to the Act step of the cycle where you analyze the work completed, you have all the information to hand.

The Plan-Do-Check-Act cycle can be implemented at any stage in your work execution plans and will help ensure continuous improvement, accelerating your maintenance team towards best-in-class, followed by world-class, maintenance execution.

*Mike Meen* is a skilled and knowledgeable professional with a proven track record of establishing the root causes of an organization's issues and delivering solutions. He has implemented value-adding programs across cultures and in a variety of industries on behalf of his customers. Most recently, Mike became chair of the competence workgroup, Step Change for Safety, delivering industry-wide guidance on competence management systems, and cocreated innovative Safety and Environmental Critical Element (SECE) verification systems (2022 Offshore Safety Award Finalist).

# BETTER MACHINE HEALTH, PERIOD.

## WI-CARE™ AS A SERVICE

 A hardware-enabled, software-as-service Predictive Maintenance delivery model backed by seasoned domain experts

 High quality data, deep analytics and actionable insights to make better asset management decisions

 Ultra-competitive pricing for ease of entry and scalability

**Start risk-free trial today**

 +1 281 940 5383

www.icareweb.com

# REPAIR OR REPLACE?
## SOME THOUGHTS
Ron Moore

A colleague recently asked if I could recommend a simple calculation applying a principle, such as Net Present Value (NPV), Internal Rate of Return (IRR), or Return on Asset Value (RAV), that could be used to determine when to replace an asset compared to just maintaining/refurbishing it. My response was that I wasn't aware of any simple ways to determine this; however, several questions need to be asked and considered while determining it. I have listed these below, along with a brief discussion of each.

## Let's start with a basic question:

What's the current asset condition? What would it cost to restore it to like-new condition and not just patch it to keep it running until the next failure? I'm assuming it's in some state of deterioration or has required repeated repairs—otherwise the question of replacing it wouldn't even be considered. Let's take that a step further and look at an example.

1. For example, if it would cost $400K to replace it and $200K to repair it, and you've lost $200K in production over the past year, along with $100K in maintenance costs/"patches" to keep it running. It seems like a pretty simple decision to replace it, especially if spare parts are difficult to obtain and/or exorbitantly expensive. If the business is closing, you will likely limp along until then. More likely, the data is not as stark as this example. So, what's the cost of the repair compared to a new one? Will that restoration give it as much life as a new one? Are parts going to be available?

2. Would the equipment benefit from a defect elimination and/or operating and maintenance practices improvement program? For example, do you understand the asset's current failure modes and consequences and how you might mitigate those? Based on this review, how much effort should be put into defect elimination and proper practices to sustain existing assets? There's little point in replacing equipment only to treat it like a rental car and replace it again within a few years. I still have my '88 Jeep Cherokee with 315,000 miles, with the original engine and drive train and no plans to replace it. Parts are becoming a problem, but it's still manageable; apparently, there is a market for parts for antiques!

3. What's expected of the asset in the next 1-, 5-, or even 10-year span? As noted, if you're closing, then limp along until you cross the finish line—don't buy anything you don't need just to get across the finish line. On the other hand, if you're growing, it may be essential to keep the asset going, including a replacement or even additional machinery, and everything in between.

4. What do you have in your budget for capital? For maintenance? If the capital budget is limited, your options are limited. If it's robust, then you need to put more thought into your options.

5. Is there new technology that makes the process or equipment much more efficient, either in its production capability, yield, cost, or quality? Does that justify a new one, even if the old one is functional at a minimum cost?

6. What's the availability and cost of spare parts for the foreseeable future? What's the impact of delays in getting the parts?

All these questions, and perhaps others, need to be answered, depending on your particular circumstance. A situational example is provided on the next page.

## EXAMPLE NO. 1

**SITUATION:** The business is stable and growing modestly. The capital budget is adequate, but with little margin. The asset is one of two critical machines in the production process. If it's down, half of the production output is lost during that period. It's 10 years old and has failed four times in the past two years, with repairs costing a total of $40,000, at $20,000 per year. Parts are available for the next five years, after which the vendor cannot guarantee their availability. There is some capability to fabricate parts through a local vendor, but at a much higher price. Production losses from those four events over two years amounted to approximately $160,000 in gross profit, at $80,000/year. A new machine is expected to cost $500,000 and, based on an engineering review, is perceived to be more reliable and easier to operate and maintain, cutting lost production and attendant maintenance costs in half. You have the capital budget for this, but should you spend it?

### Option 1—Repair

If you believe the old asset will continue to perform at its current level for the next five years, then cost twice as much to maintain into year 10, you have the following:

> **Production losses from those four events over two years amounted to approximately $160,000 in gross profit, at $80,000/year.**

Maintenance costs per year:
   $20,000/year, years 1–5;
   $40,000/year, years 6–10

Production losses per year:
   $80,000/year for 10 years

If you take this data as is, without escalating for inflation on wages and parts, or market pricing of the product, you have:

Face value annual of out-of-pocket cost + lost-production = $100,000 x 5 + $120,000 x 5 = $115,000

The Net Present Value (NPV) of this cash stream discounted @10% = $661,600

### Option 2—Replace

Maintenance costs per year:
   $10,000/year, years 1–10

Production losses per year:
   $40,000/year, years 1–10

Likewise, if you take these values at face value, you have:

Face value annual of capital cost + out-of-pocket cost + lost-production = $500,000 + $500,000 = $1,000,000

However, the NPV @10% of this cash stream is $500,000 + $306 = $806,000

Comparing the two at face value suggests replacing with a new one. However, consideration of the NPV of future improvements results in the decision to continue with the existing equipment if the market is steady or growing slightly. That may change if the future value of the product is perceived to be higher. So, what would you do?

### EXAMPLE NO. 2

Repeating most of the scenario in Example No. 1 but modifying the numbers, suppose the new asset costs $400,000, and not only do you reduce production losses, you also gain another $40,000 per year in increased production value because of the improved output and/or efficiency of the new asset. Then, the numbers work out to be:

NPV under a repair option = $661,000

NPV under a replace scenario = $400 + $306,000 – $246,000 (value of the added production) = $460,000

Therefore, you would replace the asset.

### Summary

These are just a few questions to ask and examples to consider. There are any number of other examples you could cover, but these should give you an idea of at least one approach. Ultimately, you'll want to look at the annual cost of the equipment, including maintenance and consequential costs on production (for example), then do an NPV on that cash stream for the duration of the expected use/life of the equipment. Lowest cost wins. Of course, it's okay to add to that a comparison to IRR or RAV. Note that this review does not take into account the tax benefits from depreciating the new asset and also makes a number of assumptions about inflation, markets, discount rates, etc.

In conclusion, these thoughts do not consider defect elimination or process improvement efforts to reduce the losses/costs of the existing asset. I'm a strong believer in first establishing excellence in all your practices to minimize the cost of your operation and maximize the production capability of those assets. Why should you spend more capital when you're not using the capital you have effectively?

**Ron Moore** is the Managing Partner of The RM Group, Inc., in Knoxville, TN, and provides operational excellence seminars, consulting, change management, and benchmarking services. Ron is the author of Making Common Sense Common Practice (5th ed.); What Tool? When? A Management Guide (2nd ed.); Where Do We Start Our Improvement Program?; Business Fables & Foibles; A Common Sense Approach to Defect Elimination; and Our Transplant Journey: A Caregiver's Story, as well as over 70 journal articles.

 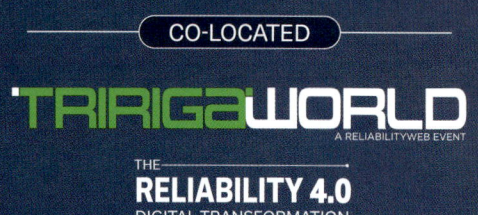

# Discover a world of innovation, information, and inspiration

- **JOIN** the largest community of Maximo® Users
- **LEARN** from the world's best run companies
- **CONNECT** with top reliability leaders and industry experts
- **EXPLORE** the marketplace of ideas

## maximoworld.com

Produced by the names you trust.

IBM® and Maximo® are registered trademarks of International Business Machines Corporation.

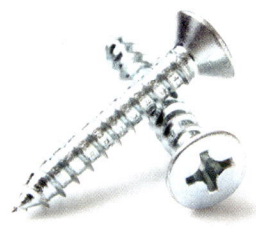

*Sometimes the smallest parts can create the biggest screw-ups.*

**Uptime is everything.** *When revenue-generating assets go down, don't get stuck without a bounce-back strategy.*

**Increased stress** on the Plant Maintenance team. Longer hours. Additional repair and maintenance costs. Putting out fires to repair critical assets over other work. It all leads to more delays and a backlog of work orders.

**Disruptions to service.** Longer wait times. Reduced quality eroding the customer experience. It all leads to decreased customer satisfaction and loyalty. In other words, lost business.

**Lost revenue.** Increased repair costs. Premature asset replacement. Decreased productivity impacting the bottom line and damaging the brand reputation, potentially leading to legal or regulatory/health safety compliance issues.

At SDI, we understand that **uptime is everything.** That's why it's critical to work with a supply chain partner to develop a **proactive strategy** to measurably minimize downtime.

Find out how SDI can help you improve uptime and reliability of critical revenue-generating assets by checking out **SDI.com**

# CRITICAL THINKING
## IN RISK-BASED DECISIONS

Brian J. Pertuit and Joseph A. DeCuir

Risk-based asset condition management programs have been around for years now, and have been a vital part of LOOP's success in our quest for operational excellence. As we strive to succeed in the crude oil pipeline industry and maintain a sound asset management program while honoring our social contract (LOOP's ESG program), we have been faced with more challenges in recent years than ever before in our company's history. To conquer these challenges, we've relied on data gathering and critical thinking to make informed, risk-based decisions. As a result, we've maintained both business continuity and the uptime of our critical assets. We believe, therefore, that this methodology has been the key to successfully navigating through adversity.

### Overcoming asset management challenges during a pandemic and back-to-back hurricanes

As LOOP and the entire world dealt with the COVID-19 pandemic, our market saw a drastic reduction in the demand for crude oil, which forced us to pivot in many aspects of our business. While we were adjusting to the early months of the pandemic, which resulted in more employees working from home, we continued to move crude oil to meet market demand and maintain our assets in new and innovative ways. Certain asset health management programs were altered to continue to monitor and maintain the condition of our assets, which required critical thinking through trying times.

Prior to resuming inspections and predictive routes, we reevaluated our criticality ranking of key assets and prioritized field integrity assessments, thermography, ultrasound, oil analysis, ultrasonic greasing and vibration routes based on current asset criticality. Due to the market downturn and how we receive and deliver crude oil these days, which is different from when LOOP was first commissioned in 1981, the operational context of many assets changed, which in turn altered the resulting criticality ranking of those assets. A reevaluation of asset condition compared to asset criticality and risks helped set the best priorities for the necessary field work.

To minimize personnel working in close proximity to one another in the field, we allowed our maintenance & reliability technicians to self-permit their work, preventing physical interaction with Operations while communication, planning and scheduling still took place remotely.

When considering risks in our asset management decisions, we also look at all associated risks from two perspectives — the risk to the organization if we don't perform the work and the risk if we do. Working remotely via web meetings, we obtained stakeholder input to risk rankings, criticality rankings, work plans, preventive maintenance procedures, scope of work documents and more to make the best decisions on the prioritization of field work to maintain critical asset uptime and business continuity while protecting people from exposure to COVID-19.

After resuming our field predictive routes and inspections, we made some great finds using airborne ultrasound to locate and prevent impending failures on a 13.8kV transfer switch and 115kV PTs in our substations. We also found high vibration signatures on some of our delivery pumps, and held web meetings to determine whether to pull those pumps or utilize other pumps in series given the lower demand. Again, critical thinking in challenging times sometimes results in not proceeding or in delaying recommended work.

Kirby P. Pierce and Arthur A. Melancon, LOOP Corrosion Specialists, perform an in-hole pipe inspection

LOOP and Strategic Partners practice social distancing during a Pre-Job Safety Kick-Off Meeting prior to performing a 115kV Substation PM at the Fourchon Booster Station near Port Fourchon, LA

Just as we were in a good rhythm and dealing with the pandemic, hurricanes Zeta and Ida hit the majority of our operating facilities and impacted most of our employees' homes over a two-year period. Damage from hurricanes of this magnitude, with over 190 mph sustained winds at peak, will cause any company with exposed field assets to become more reactive and less proactive due to the sheer volume of repairs required to maintain business continuity.

Once again, we leaned on critical thinking, risk management and cross-functional stakeholder input to prioritize our repair work in phases. When repairs were completed to a point where preventive and predictive maintenance could resume, we once again used a criticality ranking and risk-based approach to prioritize our work efforts in the field. We performed a top to bottom PM Optimization review and made significant changes to our asset health management program as a whole.

Each year, we look at the "top 20%" or the highest ranking risk to the company to prioritize and budget our work. As higher ranked risks are mitigated, they fall to the lower risk ranking reports and we then address the next highest risks. In this tiered approach, we are able to continuously move the needle by mitigating risks, thereby lowering our exposure to asset failure while preventing incidents.

> **Each year, we look at the "top 20%" or the highest ranking risk to the company to prioritize and budget our work.**

Having decades of risk management experience, Joseph A. DeCuir, LOOP's Manager of Asset Integrity, reminds us of three critical components of a robust, risk-based decision process:

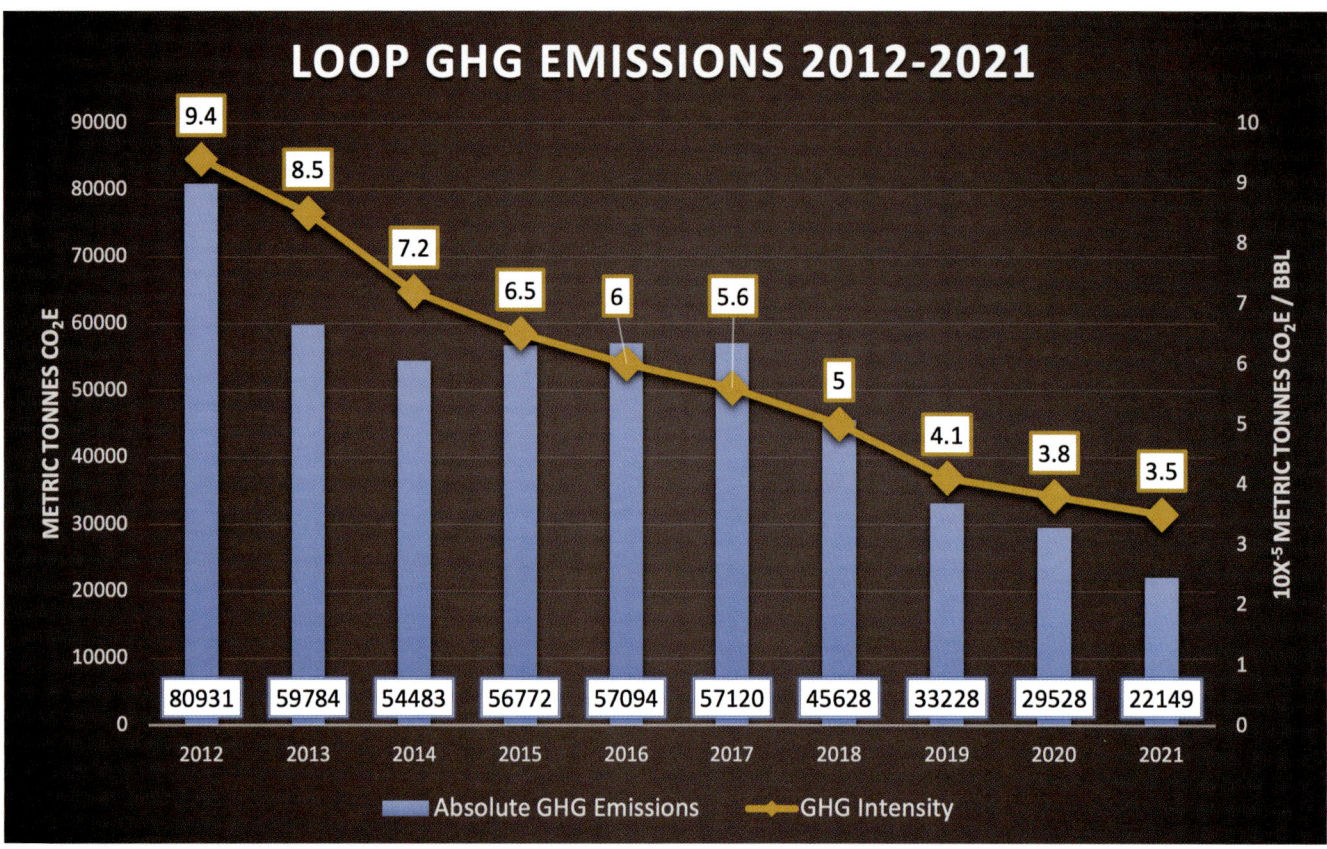

A decade of reduction in greenhouse gas emissions

❶ **When making risk-based decisions, we must consider any "unintended consequences".** This is especially true in our management of change process. Great ideas may come with consequences that were not anticipated, resulting in significant process or safety risks that must be mitigated prior to proceeding or, in some cases, may drive your decision to not proceed.

❷ **When we make risk-based decisions, we must integrate multiple data sets to verify that we are sufficiently informed about all aspects of the asset's condition before proceeding.** In large operating companies, the engineering, asset integrity, operations, maintenance and reliability programs are often overseen by multiple departments. This can create silos and stifle collaboration. We need to have a shared mindset about asset health management, which can only be achieved by collaborating cross functionally to break down silos and integrate our risk-based decision processes.

❸ **Never let a critical decision linger! No decision is a decision in itself and is almost always the wrong decision.** Make sure you invite the correct personnel with the appropriate skill sets into the conversation to make an informed decision timely, and keep an open mind to change your thinking based on any new information provided.

> # We will not lose sight of our ultimate goal of protecting the "three Ps" — People, Pipe and Planet.

### Factoring LOOP's social contract into risk-based decisions

At LOOP, we take our license to operate seriously. We call it the LOOP Social Contract, also known in the industry as our mature Environmental, Social and Governance (ESG) program. We also factor impacts to the elements of our social contract in our risk-based decision process.

The LOOP Social Contract, therefore, underpins our decisions and actions. Focusing on the future of energy is core to our mission. Today's preeminent global challenge is balancing higher energy demand from a growing population with reducing greenhouse gas emissions. As LOOP operates, we strive to cause no harm to people or the environment.

In the rapidly changing world that we live in, energy and the efficient use of natural resources play important roles. Protecting and maintaining our communities and the environment while powering our modern lifestyles is vital. The energy industry is evolving quickly as new production and competition for markets contend with shifting views on carbon and fossil fuel.

LOOP values the communities we operate in and every molecule of crude petroleum we move as an important link in the global energy supply. We continually work to ensure that our facilities operate as safely and efficiently as possible. In fact, we use far less energy today than we did 10 years ago, which has, in turn, reduced our greenhouse gas emissions significantly.

We view all forms of energy as important tools to support a growing, global population. The efficient use of crude petroleum will join renewables, such as biomass, wind, solar and alternatives, to power the world. LOOP views its role in supporting and optimizing the global petroleum marketplace as a steward in helping our communities flourish and allowing the world to use its resources in the most efficient and responsible manner possible.

> ### We continually work to ensure that our facilities operate as safely and efficiently as possible.

For LOOP to successfully advance into the future, we will be required to respond to the changing world. When we focus on our social contract and make informed decisions, we position ourselves to meet global challenges and thrive in changing environments. As we continue to implement our risk-based asset management programs and utilize critical thinking through adversity, we will not lose sight of our ultimate goal of protecting the "three Ps" — People, Pipe and Planet.

## Special Recognition

In 2021, an Environmental, Social & Governance (ESG) Performance-Based Goal Team (PBGT) of cross-functional LOOP employees was established to evaluate LOOP's legacy social contract and offer continuous improvement strategies to ensure program effectiveness. The social contract section of this article contains excerpts of LOOP's external web page (https://www.loopllc.com/LOOP-Social-Contract) further describing our ESG program, and was written as a collaborative effort by this team. Thanks to all who participated on the 2021 ESG PBGT for LOOP, and to those who are now implementing the tactical objectives derived from the strategies developed by the team.

**David A. Martin,** CMRP (d. 2018) - In the words of the late David A. Martin, CMRP, LOOP's past Reliability Planning Supervisor and coauthor of two Keeping it Simple series Maintenance & Reliability books (Lubrication 101 and Metrics/KPIs 101), we continue in our efforts to perform "the right maintenance at the right time"!

### AUTHOR

**Brian J. Pertuit,** CMRP, is a Certified Maintenance and Reliability Professional who served as the Manager of Reliability & Maintenance Planning for the Louisiana Offshore Oil Port (LOOP LLC) for a decade prior to a recent reorganization, at which time he transitioned into a Sr. Electrical Power SME role. Mr. Pertuit has over 35 years of experience in asset management, engineering and operations. He served in the U.S. Army as a Tank Mechanic Specialist (MOS 63N/63E) during overseas duty, then worked in consulting engineering as a co-op student while attending the University of New Orleans where he obtained a Bachelor of Science degree in Electrical Engineering in 1993. He has worked in the U.S. energy industry, both Oil & Gas and Power, for nearly three decades since graduating. This is his fourth article for Uptime. His past three articles were based on LOOP's Uptime Awards for Best Work Execution Management Program in 2014, Best Green Reliability Program in 2016, and Best Asset Condition Management Program in 2018.

### COAUTHOR

**Joseph A. DeCuir,** P.E., is a Professional Engineer in LA and TX and currently serves as the Manager of Asset Integrity at LOOP LLC, where he once served as the Manager of Engineering. Prior to LOOP, Mr. DeCuir also served as the Manager of Engineering for the U.S. Department of Energy Strategic Petroleum Reserve Project for 8 years. Joe's background as a subject matter expert in the areas of Pipeline Engineering, Cavern Engineering, Tank Integrity, Facility Integrity and Risk Management has supported his role over the past 10 years at LOOP to maintain and improve asset reliability by reducing risks. Mr. DeCuir has over 37 years in the Oil & Gas Industry, obtained a Bachelor of Science degree in Mechanical Engineering from the University of New Orleans in 1984 and became a registered Professional Engineer in 1996. Joe has worked on numerous API committee's since 2001, including Past Chair for the Committee on Pipeline Standards and Chair for API RP 1115 Standard for "Design and Operation of Solution-Mined Salt Caverns Used for Liquid Hydrocarbon Storage". He is presently a member of the Global Industry Services Committee for API.

Maximo Application Suite (MAS) will revolutionize enterprise asset management, but...

# YOU'RE NOT READY

MAS will catch a lot of people off guard. Don't be one of them. Transitioning to MAS requires considerable time and expertise. That's where we come in.

- Comprehensive services: assessments, installs & upgrades
- Simplified hosting with the highest level of security
- Workforce mobility via Interloc's award-winning Mobile Informer

**Scan here to learn how to get ready for MAS.**

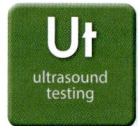

# ULTRASOUND

## For Condition Monitoring and Acoustic Lubrication for Condition-Based Maintenance

### Jim Hall

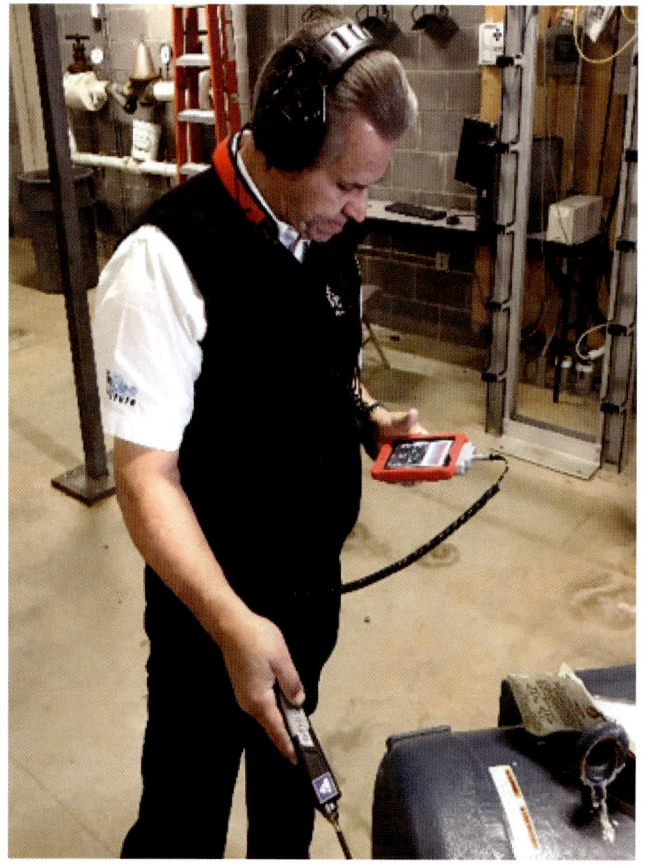

With all the hype about acoustic lubrication instruments, you would think these instruments, once turned on, would do the job for you. Far from it! Knowledge is power, but, as Albert Einstein said, "Information is not knowledge. The only source of knowledge is experience. You need experience to gain wisdom."

When implementing an acoustic lubrication program, "know" the people you are placing into this position. They must have electric motor knowledge and experience. Acoustic lubrication is more than just putting on a set of headphones and pumping grease into the bearing. It's more than just the sound of the bearing, in fact, it's only about the decibels.

**Figure 1:** Using an ultrasound instrument to trend decibel readings for trending data (Photo courtesy of The Ultrasound Institute)

## Ultrasound as a Condition Monitoring Tool

During acoustic lubrication, there is an inflection point, which is the point where the decibel goes upward or increases. Not catching the inflection point, could be the difference between over lubrication and under lubrication.

Let's use a visit to a paper mill as an example. The person performing the lubrication said the large motor required 14 ounces or one tube of grease. When asked if he thought this was too much, he replied: "No, the person who just retired had always put that amount in."

However, when asked to listen with an ultrasound instrument to the bearings he had just lubricated, he insisted the bearing must be bad after hearing a popping noise. Most of what he was hearing was the result of pumping 14 ounces of grease into the motor. Using too much grease can end up in the motor housing, blow the grease seal, push grease into the motor, causing it to overheat by insulating the windings, and possibly cause premature failure. Not to mention the internal pressure on the bearing itself.

Afterward, a visual inspection of the motor was done for grease exiting the motor casing. No grease exiting the motor was found, so he continued to think he was doing everything right.

It is not uncommon for a maintenance team to give the acoustic lubrication program to the least experienced worker. Not a mechanic, not a technician, but someone with little mechanical experience. This is a formula for disaster.

> [Acoustic lubrication] is more than just the sound of the bearing, in fact, it's only about the decibels

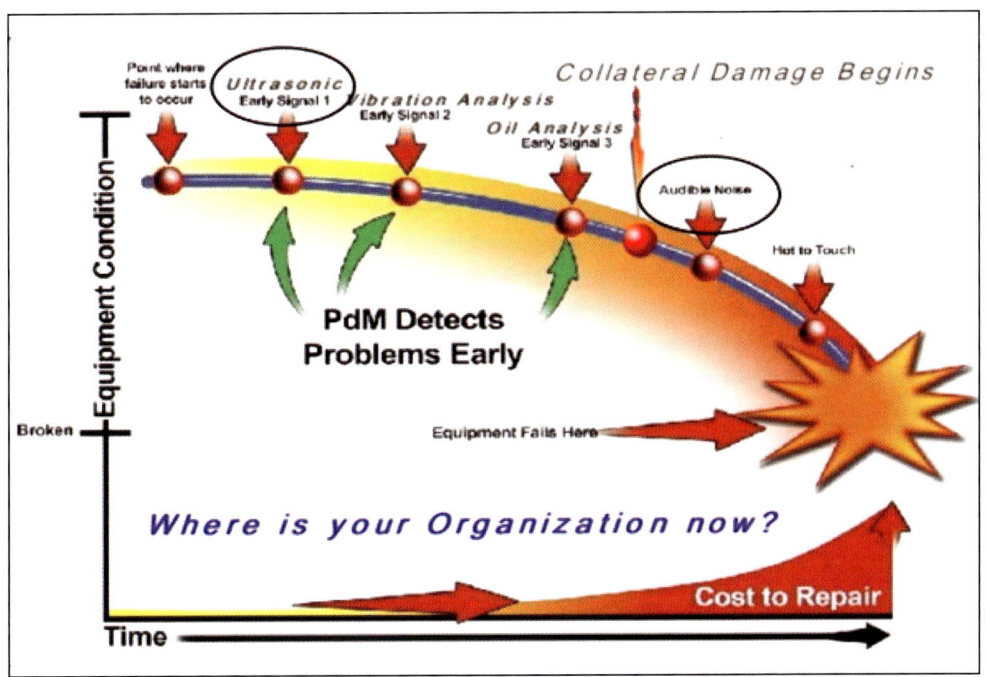

**Figure 2:** P-F curve shows ultrasound as "Early Signal 1"

Ultrasound is an excellent condition monitoring (CM) instrument. CM is a type of predictive maintenance that involves using sensors to measure the status of an asset over time during operation. With CM, maintenance is only performed when the data shows that.

Affordability, ease of use and one-point data point retrieval versus multiple points, such as vertical, horizontal and axial, are some of ultrasound's benefits. If you prefer less downtime, less man-hours lubricating motors, early detection of potential failures, less motor maintenance and less grease purchased, then implement ultrasound testing as another CM tool.

On the P-F curve, ultrasound is first to detect a defect, doing so before vibration and before infrared. Granted, because it is so early in detection, it can be very subjective. But, being too early in detection depends on the criticality of the asset being monitored.

Having vibration analysis as your primary CM tool requires having enough vibration technicians and vibration instruments to cover all your assets. Implementing ultrasound requires setting a baseline, like vibration data, and trending 30, 60 and 90 days.

## Acoustic Lubrication in Condition-Based Maintenance

Condition-based maintenance (CBM) is described as maintenance "when need arises." This maintenance is performed after one or more indicators (e.g., vibration, temperature, or decibels) show

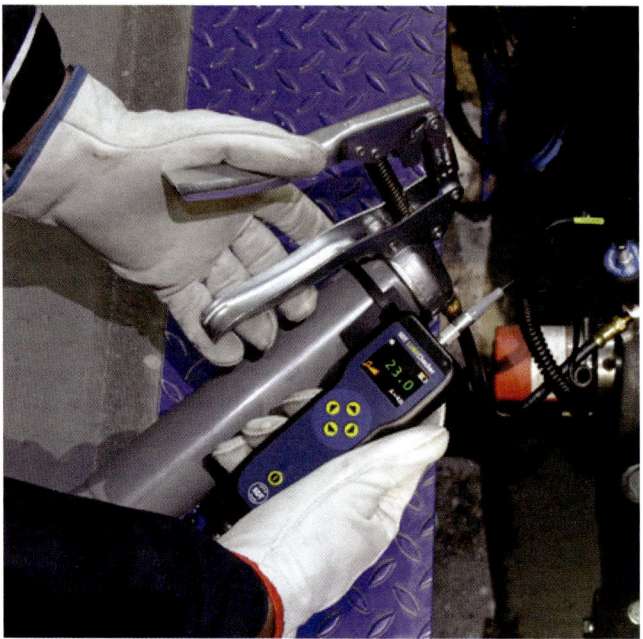

**Figure 3:** Using a grease gun with handheld acoustic lubrication instrument with decibel displayed and sensor (Photo courtesy of SDT Solutions)

that equipment performance is deteriorating or going to fail.

When trending bearings with ultrasound, once the reading is eight to 10 decibels above the previous baseline, then CBM, or you could say conditioned-based lubrication, is in order. In this case, acoustic lubrication would be the CBM.

To use an ultrasound instrument to view the decibel at the time of lubrication, you must be able to identify a beginning point. One option is the half-stroke method. As you lubricate using the half-stroke method, when the inflection point is noted, stop and give it 10 to 15 seconds to return to the decibel reading prior to the inflection point.

> **On the P-F curve, ultrasound is first to detect a defect, doing so before vibration and before infrared.**

**Figure 4:** Performing acoustic lubrication using a manual grease gun and an ultrasound instrument (Photo courtesy of The Ultrasound Institute).

(Note: In freezing or subzero weather, you may need to wait 20 to 30 seconds for the decibel to come back to the point prior to the increase.)

If the reading does not return to where it was prior to the inflection point, then stop lubricating. The half-stroke used confirms the bearing is not in need of any more lubrication. The procedure is complete. However, had the decibel dropped back to the starting point or less, another half-stroke would be warranted. Repeat this action until you reach the inflection point again.

## Why Condition-Based Lubrication?

You may be thinking: Why not simply perform a preventive maintenance (PM) action to lubricate a motor with two to three shots of grease? The answer is simple: The motor does not require any grease. It's not unusual for maintenance to have a scheduled PM requiring two to three full strokes of grease into the bearing. It's also not unusual for maintenance to put four to five pumps of grease instead of the recommended two to three pumps.

Many organizations have had great success after implementing acoustic lubrication. Your maintenance team may have experienced some hiccups implementing acoustic lubrication. But, don't get discouraged. One of the leading reasons why this practice gets dropped or is underutilized is the fear of over greasing.

Make this practice a slow and deliberate one. If using a manual grease gun, make sure you have

**Figure 5:** The button and hook setup for greasing motors, with (left) button prior to being placed over the button and (right) hook after being pulled atop button (Photo courtesy of The Ultrasound Institute)

positive pressure throughout the half-stroke of the grease gun.

There may be instances where motors require more than 10 half-strokes of the grease gun. It is important to watch the decibel of the ultrasound receiver. Watch for the inflection point or db rise in the sound level. When there is a rise or inflection of the db reading, stop and allow 15 to 30 seconds for the decibel to return to where it was prior to the inflection. If the db reading returns to its position prior to inflection, apply another half-stroke of the grease gun. Look again for the inflection point to return to where it was prior to the last increase. Once the decibel rises and does not return in 15 to 30 seconds, then you are done. Record the readings and move to the next bearing.

However, if you are performing this method of acoustic lubrication and you have completed 10 or more half-strokes and the decibel difference is not noted, then take a moment and look over the motor for signs of grease being pushed out. Look around the bearing, motor casing, grease seals, lightning holes, etc. If the motor still requires grease, then continue the acoustic lubrication practice.

Delivery of the grease is important. But, whether it's a Zerk fitting or a button and hook setup, what matters is consistent decibel readings for trending.

> ...Ultrasound can be a stand-alone tool for a large majority of your mechanical, electrical and energy maintenance and inspections

**Figure 6:** Using a grease gun with a mounted acoustic lubrication instrument with decibel displayed and sensor and Zerk fitting (Photo courtesy of UE Systems, Inc.).

Button and hook hardware is often preferable due to the strong lock and hold of the button that is threaded into the motor casing. A Zerk female adapter tends to move around when mated to the male Zerk fitting, sometimes causing inconsistent db readings. Repeatability of the decibel is important for trending purposes. You may want to discuss with upper management the removal and replacement of Zerk fittings with a button and hook setup.

Again, implementing ultrasound as a condition monitoring practice may indicate an early defect, failure, or a potential failure early on and not just a need for lubrication. Today, many maintenance departments are using vibration instruments to trend motor bearings. However, a great deal of them only have enough instruments to service a small portion of the facility's motor bearings.

Ultrasound used in a condition monitoring program can serve to offer a viable solution in two ways. First, it provides a means to detect early signs of defects, failure, or simply when lubrication is needed. Second, it determines if there is a problem beyond the need for lubrication. For example, let's say the bearing has a rise of eight to 10 or more decibels since your last report and you perform condition-based lubrication, such as acoustic lubrication. If the decibels don't go down, does that mean the bearing doesn't need any grease? Your next step, depending upon the criticality of this motor, is to put this bearing on watch. Or, possibly call for a vibration analysis of the asset.

This, too, would be condition monitoring. Whether you are using ultrasound or vibration to trend motor bearings, it is condition monitoring. In fact, ultrasound can be a stand-alone tool for a large majority of your mechanical, electrical and energy maintenance and inspections.

*Jim Hall,* CRL, *is Executive Director of The Ultrasound Institute (TUI), which specializes in training maintenance personnel in the use of airborne ultrasound equipment and the development of integrated maintenance programs.*

*Jim has worked in the ultrasound industry for over 25 years. He has attended over 350 conferences, seminars and lectures on the use of airborne ultrasound and predictive maintenance. He has the ability to provide easy and understandable information to all levels of maintenance personnel in all industries. Jim has been a contributing author to Uptime since its inception.*

# YES
# RELIABILITY
## IS **EVERYONE'S** RESPONSIBILITY

Build a culture of reliability in your team today.
Unlock lasting value for your organization tomorrow.

### www.reliabilityweb.com/events

# Achieving Trouble Free Bearing Life Through Defect Elimination

### Phil Hendrix

When a machine is designed, one of the major considerations the engineer must make is the selection of proper rolling element bearings. Some of the factors to consider in selecting bearings are shaft speeds, loads (both axial and radial), the environment they will run in, how to relube them, the duty cycle, etc. And with a few exceptions, the bearings selected for the machine should provide a trouble free life for 11 to 20 years or more. It is well known that under the right conditions, it's not unusual for some bearings to last 50 years, especially inside gearboxes where most maintenance professionals rarely get to go! There may be a lesson in that sentence. Think about it.

Figure 1 illustrates some general rules of thumb that engineers are taught to apply.

| Type of Service | Life in Hours | Equivalent Years |
|---|---|---|
| Instruments And Devices Not In Continuous Use | 500 | 1 Month |
| Equipment Used For Short Periods, E.g., Hand Tools, Etc. | 4,000 – 8,000 | 5 – 11 Months |
| Intermittent Service (Essential), E.g., Elevators | 4,000 – 12,000 | 11 – 17 Months |
| Intermittent 8 Hr Service (General Purpose) | 12,000 – 20,000 | 1.4 – 2.3 Years |
| Continuous 8 Hr Service | 20,000 – 30,000 | 2.3 – 3.4 Years |
| 24 Hour Service, Nonessential | 40,000 – 60,000 | 4.6 – 6.8 Years |
| 24 Hour Service, Essential | 100,000 – 200,000 | 11.4 – 22.8 Years |

**Figure 1:** Rules of thumb for engineers

### The Great Bearing Paradox

L10 is a term used by bearing companies that means the number of revolutions that 90 percent of a bearing population is capable of enduring before the **first signs** of metal fatigue begin to be visible under a microscope on one of its rolling elements (either races or balls). This is determined by the maximum amount of load a bearing at 33 and 1/3 rpm for 1,000,000 revolutions will endure before any signs of fatigue shows up. The L10 life is a statistical projection. An L10 life of 1,000 hours means that 90 percent of a group of identical bearings, operating in identical conditions and under the same load, should last the projected L10 hours before that first sign of metal fatigue.

Bearing experts and bearing company engineers, however, tell a different story about the "real world." They say that while this is a useful and very conservative number for design purposes, the bearing SHOULD be able to actually run 500 percent or five times that long for a useful life.

However, those in maintenance are conversely told by the SAME GROUP of bearing experts and bearing company engineers that, in the real world, these same 90 percent of bearings never even make their lower level of performance or L10, hence the "Great Bearing Paradox" that is the result of the actions by maintenance folks.

As maintenance educators teach their students, "Bearings never die of old age because

> **It is well known that under the right conditions, it's not unusual for some bearings to last 50 years, especially inside gearboxes**

AUGUST 2023   45

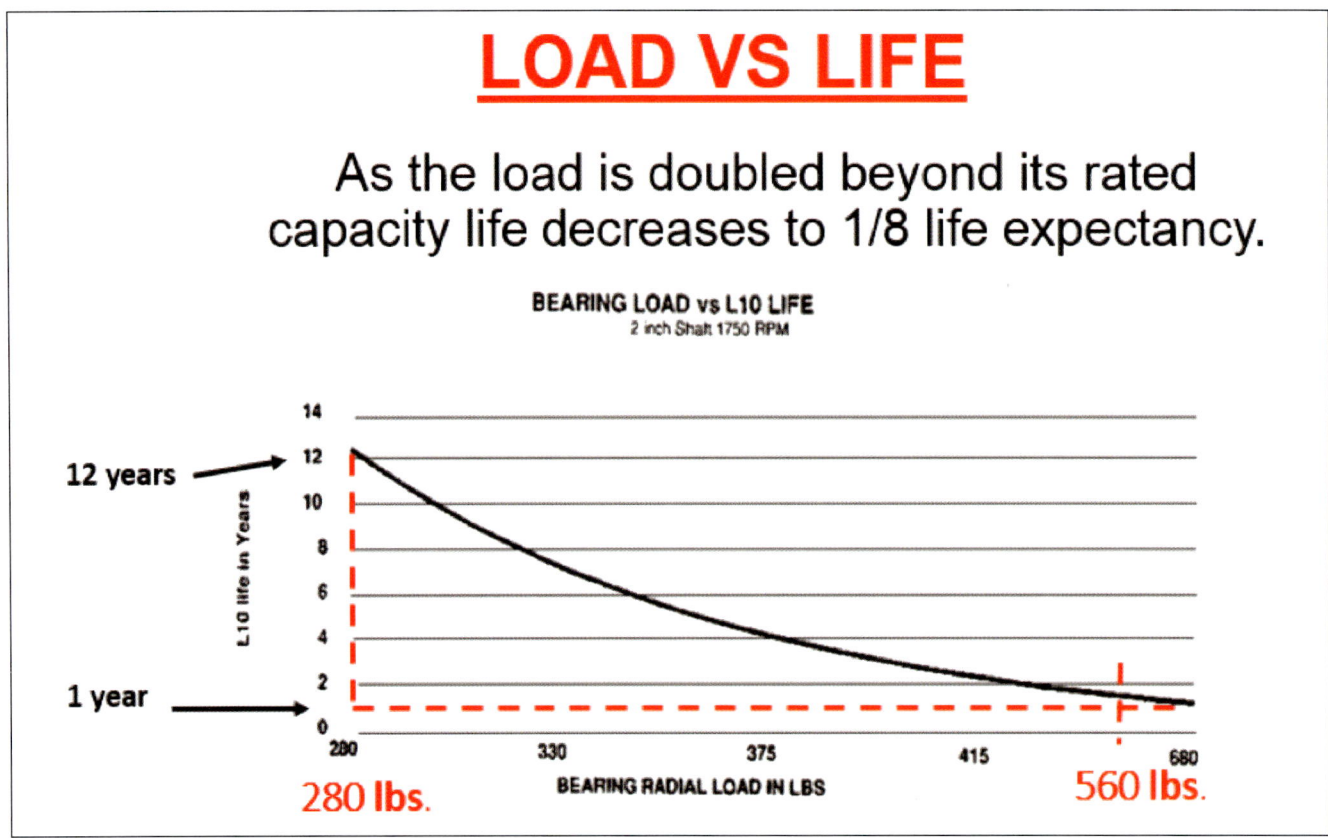

**Figure 2:** How load compromises a bearing's life expectancy

maintenance supervisors, craftspeople, operators, lubricators, stores personnel, and others continue to invent all kinds of ingenious ways to torture them, resulting in their premature death long before they achieve their L10 life expectancy!"

The graph in Figure 2 shows how increasing a bearing's load shortens L10 life as radial load is increased to a point at which the bearing is compromised. Notice that if the life expectancy is 12 years at 280 pounds of load, look what happens if that load is doubled to 560 pounds. The expected life is reduced to just under two years, an exponential reduction in bearing life.

Now, let's consider this same bearing with a speed change. If you are running it at 1,000 rpm and it has a projected similar life expectancy of 12 years, what is the impact of doubling the speed to 2,000 rpm? As you can see, the bearing life is cut in half. At 3,000 rpms, it is cut in half again, but the speed relationship doesn't nearly degrade life expectancy to the same degree as load does.

Some would argue that the mechanism of failure is not overloading the bearing material, but a reduction in oil film thickness usually brought about by unbalance or misalignment of the machine. Obviously, oil film thickness must be compromised before any metal to metal contact and subsequent overloading of the bearing material can occur.

On the other hand, others may argue that it is the actual overloading of the bearing material itself that is the primary cause of failure. At any rate,

> **L10:** The number of revolutions that 90 percent of a bearing population is capable of enduring before the **first signs** of metal fatigue begin to be visible under a microscope on one of its rolling elements.

it is clear and agreed upon that excessive loads cause premature, and too often unexpected, bearing fatigue and eventual failure.

The machine designer carefully chooses bearings that should provide adequate life for the calculated speeds and loads. Your task is not only to detect impending bearing failure and carefully analyze the symptoms of failure, but to determine and act upon the root causes using a combination of all available tools.

By doing so, you will find that many additional defects and/or assembly errors are introduced along the way, which either add additional load, compromise the lubrication, or both. Assembly by construction and/or maintenance often results in unnecessary looseness; overtightened bearings; bearing housing and shaft fit and tolerances that are just flat-out wrong (e.g., too tight or too loose); wrong length keys; pipe strain; incorrect placement of components on shafts, like belt sheaves not being as close to the bearing housing as possible; wrong lubricants; components not balanced to Grade G1.0, like impellers; missing or wrong coupling bolts; and many others. All of these factors, of course, add load and increase vibration, which eventually and often dramatically shortens the bearing life and, just as often, requires a lot of excess energy to drive the machine until failure.

## Real-Life Example

Here is a real-life example that illustrates how defect elimination and precision installs and rebuilds can enhance bearing life.

On a pump reliability improvement project, the company couldn't run a high criticality pump for six weeks between scheduled outages. In no particular order, the following problems were found:

**DEFECT 1:** The mechanics said they achieved precision alignment specs and soft foot was also checked and eliminated. Upon a careful recheck, both were found to be untrue. Realigning and eliminating soft foot resulted in a significant reduction in overall vibration, as well as a three percent reduction in electrical power usage.

**DEFECT 2:** Thrust bearings were being installed incorrectly, leaving the bearings with no preload and excess axial movement. This could have easily destroyed the impeller and/or wear plate, at a minimum. Fortunately, this was found and eliminated as the rebuilt power end was double-checked before installation.

**DEFECT 3:** The impeller, factory balanced at G1.0, was cut to a reduced diameter for the particular service pump specs and not rebalanced.

**DEFECT 4:** With pumps in this area running hot, some "rocket scientist" decided to increase the viscosity of the oil from 68 to 150 and, at the same time, with bearings running 180 to 200 degrees F, add cooling water spraying on the outside of the cast iron bearing housings, thus reducing the diameter further and the bearing clearance even more.

**DEFECT 5:** Several original equipment manufacturer (OEM) spare shafts were checked, including the one used in the rebuild, and were found to exceed the fit and tolerance dimensions from both the pump manufacturer and the bearing manufacturer at the bearing fit surface on the shaft.

**DEFECT 6:** The pump running a mechanical seal was found to have a shaft 0.002 undersized where the sleeve fits the shaft and the identification of the sleeve from a third-party supplier was found to be 0.003" too large, resulting in a sleeve to shaft fit of 0.005 total looseness. And they wonder why they can't make mechanical seals run between outages!

**DEFECT 7:** At 3,600 rpm on a 2-foot diameter shaft, they were using a set screw coupling rather than a shrink fit.

**DEFECT 8:** The same coupling was running out 0.012". Subsequent checks revealed it bored off center in a 3 jaw chuck, which every real machinist knows is the wrong way to do it!

**DEFECT 9:** Using a noted pipe strain acceptance test, both the discharge piping and the suction piping (which failed, of course) were causing the cast iron rotating power end and stainless casing to distort, putting the bearing housings out of alignment with each other.

You cannot make this stuff up! These are common problems seen all the time when doing a deep dive into a failure. If it were not so criminal, it would be funny.

## The Solution

If maintenance management would just realize the value of eliminating these defects AHEAD of starting and running rotating equipment, not only would uptime improve, but they would not have to spend so much time and money inspecting, doing vibration checks, infrared, oil analysis and, not to mention, the countless unnecessary replacements.

All of these are great and necessary tools, but they simply help you mitigate failure by hopefully scheduling an expensive and highly repetitive failure to avoid unscheduled downtime only.

*Phil Hendrix is Cofounder and Owner of Hendrix Precision Maintenance. He has 47 years of successful experience performing and leading heavy industrial maintenance in all industries. He started welding in a Fab shop at 14 years of age, which led to working construction and helping build a huge greenfield pulp & paper mill. He helped start mills up as a maintenance employee, performing every job from lubrication & millwright work on the equipment to planner, supervisor, and maintenance superintendent. After 6 years of night school, Phil obtained a Bachelor's of Science degree in Mechanical Engineering. This led to taking over four failing maintenance departments in different mills, turning each around in safety, cost, and uptime performance. Phil took an early retirement/merger buyout in 2001 to form two companies, providing hands-on Mechanical Skills Training and Predictive Maintenance Services. His passion for the last 15 years has been teaching these skills to younger maintenance people. Previous employers include Champion Paper, Simpson Paper, International Paper, and over 250 companies/plants as a Reliability Consultant and Trainer. www.hendrixprecisionmaintenance.com*

Analyze Asset Health Metrics

Minimize Operational Downtime

Optimize Asset Performance

Monitor Critical Assets

Mobilize Your Workforce

## DRIVING ASSET MANAGEMENT
# FORWARD

Let **Maven** help you drive your asset management forward.

© 2023 Maven Asset Management, Inc.

Part 1

# Bridging the Proactive Maintenance KNOWLEDGE GAP

Overcoming the Dunning-Kruger Effect

John Crossan

Despite the old saying about ignorance being blissful, there sure isn't much bliss to be seen around manufacturing plants when their maintenance folks spend their time constantly reacting to surprise equipment issues.

Ignorance is perhaps a harsh word to use, but over the years, one of the biggest obstacles I've seen to plants becoming proactive in maintenance is just that—a lack of basic knowledge about equipment care and about the processes that provide it.

Adding to the difficulty, folks without this knowledge being completely confident that they've got all kinds of it. You'll hear them say: "How hard can it be? It's just common sense."

So, if we want to spread maintenance proactivity, we need to find ways to educate folks about it, get the processes in place and then, the harder part, keeping them educated and doing those right things.

## How Big Is the Knowledge Gap?

Until they have some years of actual exposure to plant equipment in use, most people, even the technically educated, really don't understand the amount of constant care it takes to keep equipment at acceptable levels of operating performance.

(I myself was a prime example. At a tender age, suddenly ejected from a sheltered engineering cloister into the role of fledgling maintenance supervisor, inflicted on a skeptical maintenance crew, justifiably wary of a confident person who knew little of their world.)

By and large, we seem to accept equipment failure, not necessarily outright broken, just not performing like it should. It's just part of what we normally deal with. It's expected.

"Dealing with equipment issues, that's our job. It's what we do every day. It's what we're supposed to do every day. What else would we do?"

This is a big part of why overall productivity, particularly in discrete manufacturing, is well short of what it could be. We just don't expect it to be that much better.

When we routinely wait for equipment to show that it's in serious distress before we fix it, that really means it's been running in some deteriorated condition, hurting us for some time already. Reduced output, higher waste, constant quality issues, the operating difficulties we work on every day that we shouldn't have to, these things constantly frustrate and upset operators, technicians and managers, and they cost us a lot.

> …Without some years of plant experience, most people, even the technically educated, really don't understand the amount of constant care it takes to keep equipment at acceptable levels of operating performance.

Many of us too, tend to think of plant maintenance in terms of our own personal maintenance experience, our homes, our appliances and our automobiles. Generally, these pretty much need minimal care these days. Most of us don't even do that and we generally get away without many consequences.

We're pretty convinced (not unreasonably) that maintenance service, spare parts and warranty coverages are a big source of undeserved income for automobile dealers, appliance manufacturers, insurance companies, etc., and we won't buy these services unless forced to.

We'll see this in our personal items too, as either working or not working, with no in-between condition. If they're working, nothing needs to be done; if suddenly they're not working, they're repaired or replaced, usually within a day or so. The concept of continuous care to prevent performance deterioration due to wear, looseness, misalignment, etc., doesn't apply much.

But comparing with our personal items isn't valid—they don't run anywhere close to the number of continuous hours and at the stress levels that plant equipment does. They don't operate continuously in extreme heat or cold or in corrosive or vibrating environments. And we're not counting on them to consistently and cost-effectively produce a quality product that has to be continually supplied to customers to keep a company alive.

When maintenance issues come up, many operating managers in plants are faced with making decisions about something they don't know much about. And (not unreasonably) they are wary of advice from maintenance managers who might (might?) be biased, consciously or not, about the importance of equipment care versus production.

- "Do we really have to shut down for as long as they are saying?"
- "It couldn't cost that much?"

Maintenance managers are wary, also not unreasonably, of new plant accountants and managers—and the decisions they might try to make about maintenance funding and staffing.

- Folks who, without much knowledge or analysis, might say things like, "We don't seem to be having many equipment issues. We must be spending too much on maintenance."

- Attempts made to decimate the maintenance spare parts inventory according to some accounting rule of thumb, rather than basing stocking decisions on a broad-based, functional analysis.
- I remember a new plant start-up discussion, where some group members proposed, "Since all the equipment is brand new, there really shouldn't be a need to budget any funds for maintenance in the first year of operation."

And again, even technically educated engineers, unless they have spent time in plant roles, just aren't aware of many maintenance and manufacturing considerations and the pressures that go with them.

## And It's Counterintuitive

A major part of the knowledge problem is that many of the concepts around proactive maintenance aren't intuitively obvious. In fact, they're counterintuitive. They're not obvious. They're the opposite of what we would think. They're not things we'll just know automatically. They're not "simple common sense." Many aren't—it takes education and experience to "get" them.

Concepts such as:

- "Let's have our technicians spend some time on inspections rather than just repairs. That will cut down on our emergency repair work."
- "Let's take one of the technicians out of doing actual repair work and have them plan and schedule work for the others. That way we'll actually get more work done."
- "If we take some scheduled downtime for maintenance, we'll have less downtime overall."

These statements make no sense to those who have never seen these concepts working or have never even heard of them. They're a tough sell.

In criticisms of uninformed behavior, we'll often hear the statement: *"They don't know what they don't know."*

Stephen Hawking once said: *"The greatest enemy of knowledge is not ignorance; it is the illusion of knowledge."*

Also the famous, *"A little knowledge is a dangerous thing."* Albert Einstein, as with many quotes, often gets the credit for this one, but actually Alexander Pope wrote it centuries ago.

## The Dunning-Kruger Effect

So, trying to understand how smart people can confidently make decisions that keep their maintenance groups operating reactively leads us to the Dunning-Kruger effect.

Lately, there has been some media coverage of this effect, an explanation of overconfident behavior. David Dunning and Justin Kruger, professors of social psychology, noticed that consistently some students, who had done poorly on tests, somehow had great confidence that they had done really well. And, the opposite was also true; students who had done very well weren't

confident that they had done any better than others.

Dunning and Kruger built some testing around this behavior and found the results to be consistently valid. People who learned only a little about a subject suddenly believe they know a lot about it. Some were extremely confident of their knowledge. They don't know enough about the subject to realize how little they actually know about it. Then, as they learn more about the subject, people realize the actual size and complexity and become less confident of how much they actually know.

Even worse, Dunning and Kruger found that this behavior isn't something that's just true of "them," those imperfect ones among us. Sadly, it's true of all of us, another of those unfortunate characteristics of being human. Some are just louder than others. We all have to realize that we can behave this way and compensate for it.

And it seems that we see this more and more around us every day, with so much information now presented by media in short, simple sound bites with no depth. People are opinionated and passionate about issues they know little about and only listen to one simple perspective on it.

Those who have learned more, whose perspectives are broader, are usually more balanced— realizing that the issues aren't that simple and can't be simply resolved.

This also explains, but certainly doesn't excuse, some of the noxious, polarized opinions that sadly we've all heard at times in maintenance discussions in plants. These happen when folks haven't taken the time to understand issues and don't make efforts to constantly communicate with each other.

Managers and supervisors saying maintenance issues are simply due to a maintenance group that's mostly "lazy, uncaring, incompetent, arrogant" and "somebody needs to get after those guys."

Maintenance folks insisting that managers "only care about cost and production numbers and nothing else" and "can't be bothered to know or care about maintenance issues."

### What to Do?

So, if we recognize that not knowing enough about maintenance really isn't making us blissful, then how can we get our plants educated about the amount of care our equipment needs and the processes to best provide it?
Then, the harder part, how can we keep everybody educated and keep ourselves doing these right things in the right way?

We'll talk particularly about this harder part in part 2 of the article.

***John Crossan*** consults in manufacturing and maintenance improvement and has spent over 40 years with major companies in operations and engineering. For much of the last 14 years, he has focused on improving operations by fostering the installation and ongoing implementation of basic manufacturing and maintenance processes, incorporating lean concepts, across some 30 varied plants in the U.S. and Canada. John is currently working on a book covering the basics of proactive maintenance systems that emphasizes the human factors that influence its acceptance and sustainability. www.johncrossan.com

# 13 Project Management Fundamentals

## to Support Successful CMMS-EAM Optimization Projects

Jason Weis

As maintenance organizations mature, so should their applications that support their asset management processes. Activities should be optimized along with supporting technologies to eliminate wasteful tasks and focus on value-added activities. Continuous improvement should be part of every organization and every department. This is where optimization projects come into play. Computerized maintenance management systems (CMMS) and enterprise asset management (EAM) systems of today are highly configurable to meet the business requirements of the customer. This is a great feature if the proper controls, guidance and a strategic plan for a future state are in place. If they are not, the business will find itself in a costly hole it didn't realize was being dug.

Optimization projects, business process changes, and version upgrades keep the system operating effectively and reliably. As the organization matures, people also learn how functionality not currently being used can be leveraged to gain efficiencies while becoming more effective managing work processes, inventory, spare parts, preventive maintenance jobs, etc., Plans can be put in place to implement the necessary changes to take advantage of these improvements. Many of these projects fail for the same reasons all projects fail, weak project management, lack of planning, absence of sponsorship, poor communication, inadequate change management, and not understanding what a successful project will look like at the end. Businesses must know how to manage and what to manage to improve project success rates and bring real value to the organization.

The following 13 project management fundamentals must be in place to ensure the success of any optimization project.

## #1: Project Management

"Trying to manage a project without project management is like trying to play a football game without a game plan," says Karen Tate, president and founder of The Griffin Tate Group, Inc. (TGTG), a Project Management Institute (PMI) Charter Global Registered Education Provider specializing in training for the project management community. Quality project management is key to the success of any project. Project management is led by the project manager (PM), who is responsible for advanced planning to manage the project's time, cost and performance as it moves

> **Trying to manage a project without project management is like trying to play a football game without a game plan.**

forward. The PM is responsible for managing the five phases of a project: initiating, planning, executing, monitoring and controlling, and closing the project. Each of these phases include activities that use inputs and tools and techniques to generate outputs. The PM is like the quarterback, ensuring the proper planning occurs for all the phases to support the effective execution of the activities.

An experienced PM is familiar with the required inputs and outputs of activities and the tools and techniques used to generate deliverables from activities that will be used throughout the project. PMI describes project management as, "The application of knowledge, skills, tools and techniques to project activities to meet project requirements." PMI goes on to say, "Project management enables organizations to execute projects effectively and efficiently."[1] A lack of PM experience and methodologies can spell disaster in the forms of budget overruns, scheduling issues, and costly rework that also frustrates and demoralizes team members.

## #2: Project Charter

The project charter (PC) is created in the initiating stage of a project. The PC is the first document for the project that needs to be signed off on before proceeding with project activities. According to the PMI, "The project charter establishes the partnership between the performing and requesting organizations."[2] The PC is usually created by the project manager and includes items like the project scope, objectives, success criteria, required resources, budget, known risks, stakeholders, etc. Keep it concise and to the point, about one page. Consider it an executive summary to a specific audience to sell the project.

The project sponsor signs off on the project charter after reviewing it with the PM and making any necessary revisions. Once signed, the document signifies the existence of the project. From the very beginning of project initiation, the project charter serves as a reference to help stakeholders understand the vision of the project. It should be presented in the project's kickoff meeting with the project sponsor present to support the document and answer any questions. All stakeholders present at the kickoff meeting should have a clear understanding of the project after the PC is presented.

## #3: Project Sponsor

An effective project sponsor supports the project manager and the overall success of a project. This person is the highest level of management on the project. The project sponsor has the authority to allocate funds and resources and helps define the project, break down barriers and champion the project through good and bad. Engagement from the sponsor conveys the importance of the project's vision and goals to department managers and the folks from their respective departments assigned to the project. The project sponsor and project manager work as a team, ensuring the project stays on track.

Never underestimate the power of presence of the project sponsor in project meetings. It is important for the team to see the sponsor engaged. When the sponsor supports the mission of the project and recognizes the work the team is putting into the project, it encourages team members and managers to put forth their best efforts.

## #4: Project Oversight Committee

The project oversight committee (POC) is a team of department leaders that have a stake in the project. These folks are on the team because the project will have a direct impact on them or their direct reports are assigned to the project team. Project phase and complexity help dictate how often this group needs to meet. The PM provides project updates to the POC, keeping them informed on the status of the project and especially when sign-offs are required on documents and deliverables.

Since the PM on the CMMS project probably has little authority over the project's team members, the POC should help prioritize project activity and deliverables to remain on schedule. Department managers on the POC also help drive amicable decisions when the project team cannot agree on a path forward. If the POC cannot come to an agreement, the issue then can be escalated further up the chain to the project sponsor. The POC also supports the sustainability of the change. The proper training and tools should be provided for them to support the change post implementation. Don't leave them hanging and expect these managers to do this on their own.

## #5: The Project Team

Project success and quality of deliverables are constructed on the experience and knowledge the project team possesses and how well they work together. These folks should be the subject matter experts (SME) in their functional role. To be effective, these team members must learn to collaborate as a cohesive group and be willing to listen to new ideas while treating their team members with respect. It takes time for teams to begin to perform together. The phases the teams go through are described by psychologist Bruce Tuckman as: forming, storming, norming and performing. How fast or slow the team moves through these stages varies and sometimes the team may even regress. Learn these stages and how to help lead the team through them.

How knowledgeable the SME from each department is makes a difference. The more experience team members have with the application and business processes, the more accurate and effective the process mapping exercise will be. In addition, the more familiar people are with best practices in their area of specialization, the more ideas they will be able to contribute. These participants may even be aware of functionality not being used and may have some thoughts about how to leverage these features to improve business processes.

## #6: Communicate Effectively

Effective communication may be the single most important aspect of management, period. This is especially true with projects. Project activities can fail due to misunderstandings and ineffective communications as people may think they are doing the right thing, what they thought was communicated to them. Irish playwright George Bernard Shaw once said, "The single biggest problem in communication is the illusion it has taken place." Effective communication keeps project team members at all levels informed of assignments, progress, expectations, decisions, schedule changes, etc. The more effective the communications, the more engaged team members will be.

The balance with communication lies in the right communications and the level of detail to the right stakeholders with the right frequency. Planning a project communication plan will indicate who needs to know what and on what frequency. It helps to know what types of communication work in your organization and what does not. Review communication methods and build a plan. People cannot help correct issues or be engaged with the project if they are not informed. Do not expect people to go searching for different types of project documents; they may not even know they are available to be viewed. Plan your communications to ensure the right project information is received by the right people at the right time.

## #7: Common Language

Similar words mean different things to different people and this is particularly true when referring to objects, items, or things in different systems. This can also be referred to as semantic noise. It is a common issue when bringing people together that do their work in different systems or applications. Wikipedia says semantic noise occurs when, "The sender of the message uses a word or a phrase that we don't know the meaning of, or which we use in a different way from the speaker". When the cross-functional team gathers, it is important for the facilitator in meetings to pay special attention to the words people from different departments are using and what they are implying. Focus on building a common language for the project where everyone understands the meaning of words specific to the application the project is focusing on.

Don't assume someone understands what you are saying to them, be sure to elaborate, especially early in the project. Project managers facilitating meetings should listen intently to not just hear the words people say, but what they are trying to communicate to the rest of the team. If project managers have any doubt or notice any team members looking like they do not clearly understand what is being said, they should intervene. Don't call anyone out, simply ask some questions, allowing more details to be provided about what is being communicated. From process mapping to requirement gathering, the team's understanding of application-specific terms will improve.

## #8: Verify the Current Business Processes

The current business processes should be known before starting a project. If you do not know the current processes, it will be nearly impossible to determine the correct scope and where to start the project. Business process mapping workshops should be held with the project team to review the current documented processes and ensure their accuracy. If they are not documented, document them. Undocumented changes from the past can be captured here to ensure everyone understands the process from beginning to end. If they are documented, verify them.

Next, the team should talk through the process and map it from beginning to end. Everyone on the cross-functional team gains a more in-depth understanding of activities up and down stream of where they fit into the process. The team can learn how small adjustments for the way they do their job can have a positive impact on coworkers downstream in the process. It can be an eye-opening experience for people from different departments who are not aware of various departments' functions and roles. Process mapping helps identify process gaps and uncovers root causes of issues and presents opportunities for improvements.

## #9: Project Assessment

A vendor assessment combined with the business process mapping exercise helps to understand what you are getting into when planning a project. Lack of knowledge on the existing system, functionality and potential customizations can spell disaster for the project before it begins. Benjamin Franklin once said, "By failing to prepare, you are preparing to fail." With regard to projects, this quote is right on point. Consider having the vendor you are partnered with perform an assessment on the current status of the application. The cost of the assessment will likely be less than the costs the project would incur without the assessment. The vendor should gain a detailed understanding of the technical build and how it drives functionality and get to know stakeholders through interviews.

There will be surprises during the project, however, with the right planning and prework, they can be reduced significantly. Knowledge is power. Decisions based on intelligence typically turn out better than decisions based on assumptions. Learn as much as possible preparing for the project, allowing decisions to be based on intelligence. With the vendor's expertise and knowledge of your system environment after the assessment, they will be able to help guide the business toward opportunities for improvements.

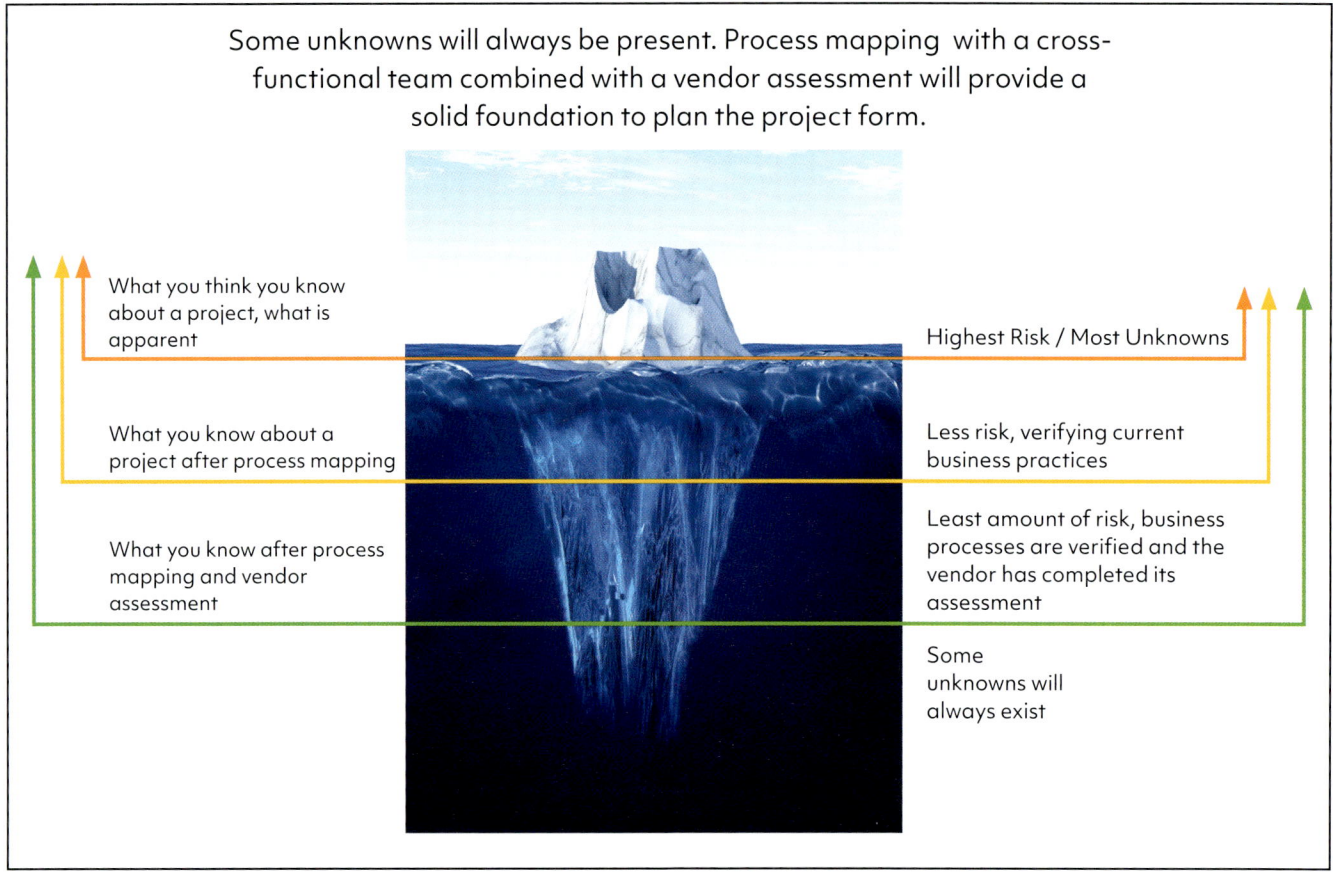

**Figure 1:** Process mapping as part of the project assessment helps uncover the unknowns

## #10: Desired Future State – Know the End Game

To identify the desired future state, define what the business is looking to gain from the project, understand what problem is being solved and the root causes of the issues. Whether it is achieving greater technical reliability, leveraging additional system functionality, or eliminating non-value-added activities from work processes, know what the end goals are. Hopefully, the project exists because it is a piece of the strategic asset management plan. If there is no strategic asset management plan or long-term project portfolio plan to reference for guidance for improvements, take a look at ISO55000 to learn more about structured asset management methods and frameworks. According to Distinguished Marine and WWII Medal of Honor recipient Woody Williams, "No matter how good the team or how efficient the methodology, if we're not solving the right problem, the project fails."

A properly planned and managed project is like planned maintenance work. The proper "things" are planned in advance of the job, ensuring everything is in place to execute the job when it is coordinated and scheduled with operations to be completed. In contrast, there is reactive or emergency work. Emergency work is not planned, interrupts planned activities, costs more, can increase overall risk of the job, and rework might even be required. The "fix" may not be ideal, but you do what you can to mitigate the immediate problem "good enough" at the time. You do not want your project to be "good enough" or cause interruptions to other planned work. Sometimes it helps to start from the end, work backward from what the project should look like when completed. This provides another perspective of how to get to that end game.

## #11: Sustainable Change and Change Management

Biologist Charles Darwin may not have been thinking about managing projects and change management when he said, "It is not the strongest of the species that survives, nor the most intelligent that survives. It is the one that is the most adaptable to change." However, this perspective also applies to businesses adapting to changing environments as needed to remain competitive. Change isn't easy. To be better prepared to manage the change, consider the organization's readiness to accept change. Regarding change management, the PMI states, "When an organization identifies the type of change needed and chooses a change process, the next step is to understand the culture and political environment in which the change will occur."[3]

When people don't understand the value of change or the change is not a direct benefit to them, they will put little effort into supporting it. Some people will even put efforts into circumventing the change. This is why employee engagement, communicating the value of the change to those affected, and supporting the change with effective change management strategies, including ongoing training, are key to sustainable change. Keep in mind change isn't always good for everyone involved. In some instances, jobs may be eliminated with process improvements and gained efficiencies. These are the more delicate changes that need to be managed with care. Absence of a change management plan will drastically reduce acceptance and how effective the project is after implementation.

## #12: Vendor Partnership

Vendors are the people who possess expertise of the system. Building a good relationship with them will help when their expertise is called upon by the business to support improvement projects. An ongoing relationship turns into a partnership where both parties benefit. People will get to know each other and learn to work together, just like the folks on the project team. If you have a support contract with a vendor, stay in touch with them. There should be an open line of communication between the vendor and the person responsible for administering the application.

Listen to the vendor, they have your best interests in mind. And for the vendors, listen to the customers. Vendors want to be part of a successful project as much as the business needs the project to succeed. Both parties should talk out available options for solutions with an open mind. In most cases, vendors are able to present more than one option for how improvements can be made. As the saying goes, there's more than one way to skin a cat. Review proposed solutions, discuss them and select the one that makes the most sense for the business and the people.

## #13: Business Analysis

PMI summarizes business analysis as, "The set of activities performed to identify business needs and recommend relevant solutions; and to elicit, document and manage requirements."[4] The internal business analyst, if there is one, or members of the project team are tasked with making project recommendations based on facts and supporting evidence. Vendors know specific application

functionality, however, the business analyst and or team provides recommendations for how additional functionality can be leveraged to gain advantages for the business. "As organizations begin to recognize how to use business analysis to their competitive advantage, there is an increasing demand for practitioners with the required business analysis skills."[5]

Analysis should go beyond the current project and consider the portfolio of applications and future planned projects for those applications. The business analyst may be aware of higher level initiatives that department SMEs are not. In some cases, new integrations may be required to share data between different applications to improve effectiveness and data sharing. The business should put effort into avoiding change that will impede future improvements. Tactical changes should not hinder future strategic changes. Proper business analysis will help avoid these situations where efforts and money is wasted on a change that will later need to be removed or reversed.

## Summary

As the great baseball player Yogi Berra said, "If you don't know where you are going, you might end up somewhere else." Solid project management methods and organizational sponsorship are the keys to success. Know where your project needs to go, do the planning and create the road

Jason Weis, PMP

map to guide the project and the team to move it forward methodically.

- Assign the right project manager.

- Establish the project organization from top to bottom, including the project manager, project sponsor, project oversight committee and cross-functional team.

- Create the project charter to define the project and have the project sponsor sign off on it.

- Be aware of tactical and strategic initiatives when making decisions.

- Know the end game, what the project will look like in the end when it is a success.

- Develop a common language and communicate effectively.

- Leverage project hard gates for sign-offs before proceeding.

- Do the planning for all phases of the project.

- Build a solid relationship with a vendor and the project team; you all want to be successful.

- Business analysis is critical to fixing the right things, the right way.

- Create a sustainability plan.

## References

1. Contributors, W. (2023, April 6). *Communication Noise*. Retrieved from Wikipedia the Free Encyclopedia: https://en.wikipedia.org/wiki/Communication_noise
2. Project Management Institute. (2013). *Managing Change in Organizations: A Practice Guide*. Newtown Square: Project Management Institute, Inc.
3. Project Management Institute. (2015). *Business Analysis for Practitioners: A Practice Guide*. Newtown Square: Project Management Institute, Inc.
4. Project Management Institute. (2017). *A Guide to the Project Management Body of Knowledge: PMBOK Guide*. Newtown Square: Project Management Institute, Inc.
5. Project Management Institute. (2021). *A Guide to the Project Management Body of Knowledge 7th Edition*. Newtown Square: Project Management Institute, Inc.

*Jason Weis* worked on several commercial and industrial construction projects as a Journeyman Electrician. He also worked as an Instrument Technician in nuclear generation plants, coal burning power plants, and helped restart the Delaware City and Monroe Energy refineries as a contractor. He has extensive experience both in the field and in planning and scheduling, asset management and Project Management. In addition to completing a 5 year IBEW apprenticeship Jason also earned a bachelor's degree in construction management, and the following certifications - PMP, CRL and CMRP.

# Strategic Maintenance Management Course
## Rapid Acquisition of Business Process Knowledge for Maintenance Leaders

**SMM — STRATEGIC MAINTENANCE MANAGEMENT COURSE**

## 18 MODULES

1. Roles and Responsibilities of a MM/ML
2. Expectations and Requirements
3. Gaining Stability and Control
4. Doing the "Right" Work
5. Doing the "Work" Right
6. Lifecycle Management (10 Rights)
7. Preventive Maintenance
8. Work Processes
9. CMMS
10. MRO Inventory and Purchasing
11. Aligning to the Organizational Objectives
12. Information and Knowledge
13. Training Programs
14. Intangible Assets
15. Financial Assets
16. Regulatory Compliance
17. Operator Driven Reliability
18. Continuous Improvement

www.reliabilityweb.com/events

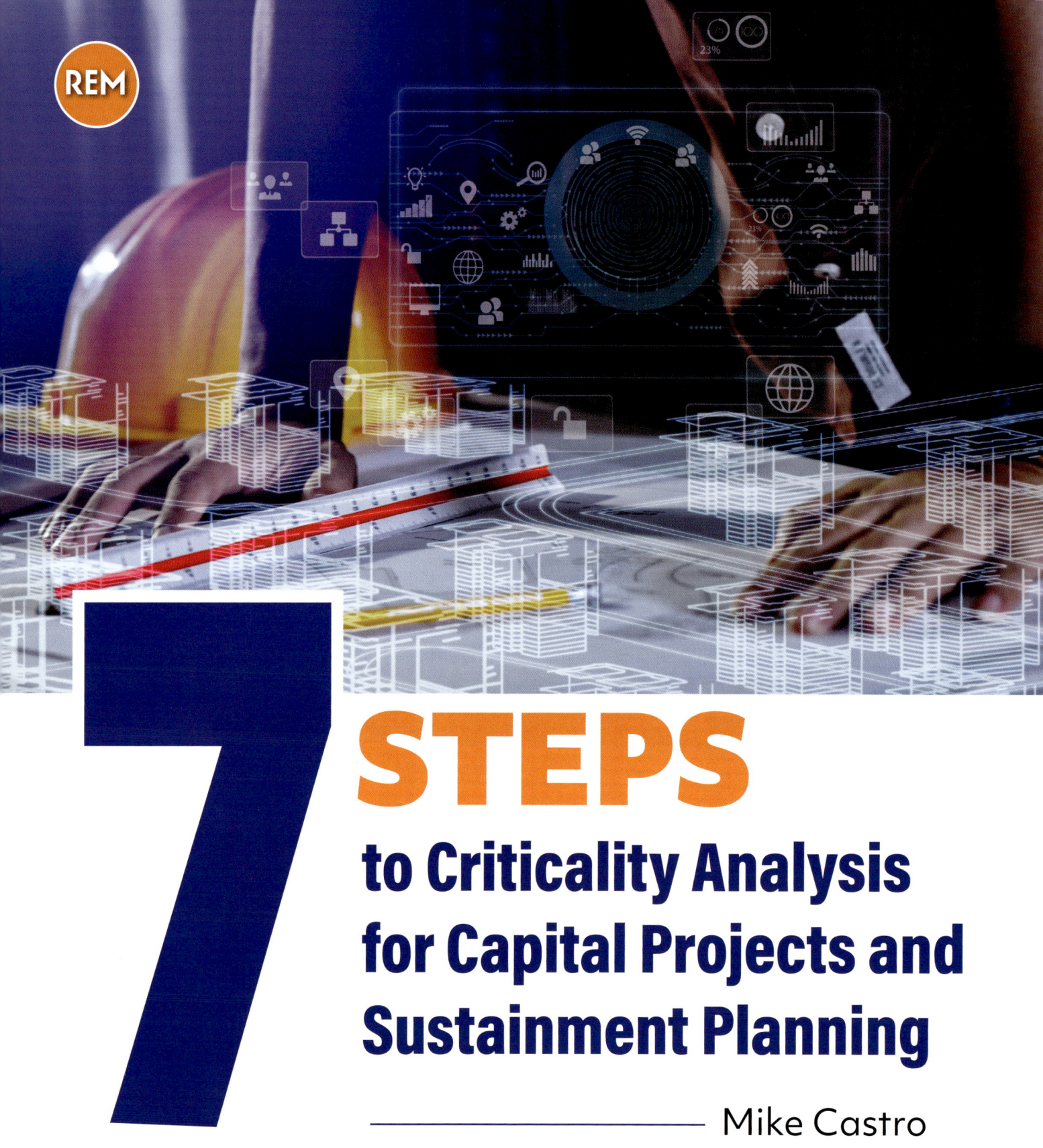

# 7 STEPS
## to Criticality Analysis for Capital Projects and Sustainment Planning

— Mike Castro

# How to Perform a Criticality Analysis for Capital Planning and Sustainment Planning

Asset criticality is a ranking of assets according to potential operational impact. This is usually determined through a formal asset criticality analysis on each asset or group of like assets.

The analysis is based on agreed upon criteria, such as safety, environmental and quality risks; operational impact (e.g., supply chain, demand, profitability, etc.), mission impact, maintenance and reliability impact (e.g., consequence and severity of failure), level of redundancy, asset replacement cost, spare lead time, or any other factor important to an organization.

Criticality supports prioritization of assets that are important to monitor and should be maintained at an agreed upon level of maintenance based on the consequences of failure.

A well-defined asset criticality analysis helps to improve:

1. Capital projects and sustainment planning
2. Maintenance optimization
3. Work order prioritization
4. Cost avoidance metrics

## STEP 1
### Define the Scope

Define which assets will receive criticality analysis and which will not. All assets may not benefit from a formal analysis. For example, it may be advantageous to limit the scope to only assets with an active preventive maintenance plan, only assets owned by a particular organization or contained in buildings of higher importance, or only assets of a particular type, such as building assets and not vehicles. Once the number of assets is settled, the time for completion needs to be agreed upon. Completion time depends on several factors: How in depth the scoring will be, how many staff hours can be dedicated to the effort, how experienced the team is, etc. As a very rough estimate of time, you can assume it will take one minute of time per asset.

The first step relies on the integrity of your asset registry. An asset registry is a list of all assets that may be stored in a computerized maintenance management system (CMMS) or in a spreadsheet. If your organization does not have a registry and merely maintains equipment as it breaks down, a list will need to first be created. Similarly, a registry may exist, but is so outdated/incorrect that it is unusable. To create/correct an asset registry, each asset needs to be logged, either in person or using reliable reference material such as building drawings. This is also a good time to capture information necessary to perform the criticality assessment, such as nameplate data and equipment configuration.

## STEP 2
### Form a Team

Determine the stakeholders for criticality, then hold regular meetings to confirm the rating. All positions could be from within an organization if self-performing, or, if applicable, a mix of contractors and organization members. A typical team consists of a:

- **Criticality Leader** – This person is the leader of the effort, driving the project through completion. Responsibilities include coordinating regular meetings, updating the spreadsheet or whatever tool is used, collecting information vital to the analysis, and putting the first pass of a score on each asset.

- **Asset Owner** – The owner or representative of the asset owner who typically has the heaviest weight on the final asset criticality score.

- **Subject Matter Expert** – An individual who best understands the function of the asset and how it is related to other equipment. Typically, the responsible maintenance technician (i.e., the person who fixes the asset when it's broken), maintenance supervisor, operator, or someone who has just been around for a long time and knows the assets, can fill this role. This individual will likely rotate depending on what group of assets are being looked at.

- **Safety** – An individual who is or can act as the safety representative in a maintenance organization. This person should seek to give extra consideration to assets failures that pose a life safety hazard.

- **Planner/Scheduler/Production Control (optional)** – This individual or team performs planning, scheduling and jointly manages the CMMS system. These people typically have a strong understanding of asset configurations and provide great value to the criticality scoring team. They can also advise on how best to integrate the score into the CMMS.

- **Executive Sponsor (optional)** – This individual can help direct resources to the project and has an interest in its success. The resources may be financial and/or personnel related.

## STEP 3
### Define Criteria

How to score each asset needs to be defined by the group. Presented here are three criteria examples that can be referenced and modified to best fit the facility being analyzed. The team must define and agree on a criticality ranking process that is valuable, usable, and understandable to all stakeholders. An example is the criticality method outlined in the NASA Procedural Requirements, NPR8831.2F. The criteria table is shown in Figure 1.

Another popular and simple scoring system is High, Medium, Low. ISO14224: Petroleum, petrochemical and natural gas industries — Collection and exchange of reliability and maintenance data for equipment has a failure consequence block, provided in Figure 2, that can be used to score assets. Using the table in Figure 2, High could be

| Criticality | Criteria |
|---|---|
| 1. | Environment, health, safety impact with a single point of failure. |
| 2. | Mission impact, single point of failure. |
| 3. | Environment, health, safety impact, multiple failures required. |
| 4. | Mission impact, multiple failures required. |
| 5. | Center impact (nonmission). |
| 6. | Significant economic consequences. |
| 7. | Employee morale. |
| 8. | Public Relations. |

**Figure 1:** One criticality criteria example is NASA's NPR8831.2F

| Consequences | Category | | | |
|---|---|---|---|---|
| | **Catastrophic**<br>Failure that results in death or system loss | **Severe**<br>Severe injury, illness or major system damage | **Moderate**<br>Minor injury, illness or system damage | **Minor**<br>Less than minor injury, illness or system damage |
| Safety | I<br>• Loss of lives<br>• Vital safety-critical systems inoperable | V<br>• Serious personnel injury<br>• Potential for loss of safety functions | IX<br>• Injuries requiring medical treatment<br>• Limited effect on safety functions | XIII<br>• Injuries not requiring medical treatment<br>• Minor effect on safety function |
| Environmental | II<br>Major pollution | VI<br>Significant pollution | X<br>Some pollution | XIV<br>No, or negligible, pollution |
| Production | III<br>Extensive stop in production/operation | VII<br>Production stop above acceptable limit$^a$ | XI<br>Production stop below acceptable limit$^a$ | XV<br>Production stop minor |
| Operational | IV<br>Very high maintenance cost | VIII<br>Maintenance cost above normal acceptable$^a$ | XIII<br>Maintenance cost at or below normal acceptable$^a$ | XVI<br>Low maintenance cost |

$^a$It is necessary to define acceptable limits for each application.

**Figure 2:** A high, medium, low criticality criteria example from ISO14224

| Crit # | Description |
|---|---|
| 5 | Critical safety-related items and protective devices |
| 4 | Critical to continued production of primary product |
| 3 | Ancillary (support) system to main production process |
| 2 | Standby unit in a critical system |
| 1 | Other ancillary assets |

**Figure 3:** A 1-5 criticality criteria example from *Asset Maintenance and Reliability Best Practices*

reserved for quadrants I, II and V, Low reserved for quadrants XII, XV and XVI and Medium would represent the remaining quadrants.

Finally, a simplified 1 through 5 asset criticality referenced in the book, *Asset Maintenance and Reliability Best Practices, 3rd Edition* by Ramesh Gulati, is provided in Figure 3.

## STEP 4
### Grouping and Scoring

Scoring assets individually can be a time-consuming process if there are a significant number of assets. Instead of scoring each one, similar assets can be assigned to a group and that group can be scored. For example, all the fire alarm panels for a building could be lumped into a single group and given the same score. Groups of assets should share the same service and consequences of failure.

When starting to score assets, the ones that are obviously critical or obviously noncritical are

| Group | Crit. | Group Description | Function/Service | Subject Matter Expert | Amount in Group |
|---|---|---|---|---|---|
| Doors | 5 | Entrance doors, hanger doors, roll up doors | Access to building | Andrew C. | 171 |
| Pump, HVAC, MDI 1-3, without redundancy | 2 | Chilled, condenser, or hot water supply, return, or recirculating pumps without known redundancy, known single point of failure, or only one in building, in MDI critical, significant, or relevant rated buildings. | Chilled, condenser, or hot water to HVAC type equipment. | Mike C. | 171 |
| Gym Equipment | 7 | Motorized divider curtain, basketball goal, bleachers, sauna heaters | Various equipment serving the fitness center | Travis G. | 17 |

**Figure 4:** Grouping and scoring spreadsheet example

easier to begin with as the team becomes familiar with their scoring criteria and the scoring process. These are typically life safety systems and equipment directly serving the goals of an organization. Noncritical equipment examples include bathroom exhaust fans, kitchen equipment, drinking fountains, etc. Using this method, approximately half of your assets can be quickly grouped and scored and allow the team to make some early progress.

The other half of your assets are typically for equipment with hard to define service areas. Think about electrical panels. For a large site, there could be thousands of electrical panels, the services of which are not exactly known without going through thousands of schedules and drawings. For these, it can be helpful to define how critical the individual buildings or rooms are, then determine which assets serve those spaces. For example, the consequences of failure for HVAC systems in more critical buildings would be higher than a similar system in a less critical building.

An example spreadsheet for grouping and scoring is provided in Figure 4. In a separate tab of the spreadsheet, each asset would be assigned its relevant group.

## STEP 5
### Meet Regularly

The criticality leader should regularly go through the assets on the list and assign a temporary criticality number using the agreed upon method. Assuming the tool used to track criticality is a spreadsheet computer program, the temporary number would be highlighted yellow to indicate its temporary status. During the meeting, the leader would then present the recommended number to the stakeholders. The number would be approved or changed, then updated to green to indicate a complete status. If the number is not agreed upon or more information is needed, the color remains yellow and is brought up again at the next meeting. The subject matter expert generally rotates, as a new expert is asked to join depending on what asset category is on the agenda. For example, if the agenda for the week lists plumbing assets, it would be helpful to invite the plumber who maintains them. By repeating this process, all assets will receive an approved rating and the team can more easily report on progress and estimate time until completion.

## STEP 6
### Updating the Asset Registry

The final scoring should be placed back into the asset registry or CMMS database. If using enterprise asset management (EAM) software, some have a built-in "priority" field that can be utilized. Alternatively, the "priority" display name can be changed to criticality or a new field can be added. It is best to rely on the expertise of the team's optional Planner/Scheduler/Production Control Person on how best to update the system.

Once the information is properly stored in the maintenance database, it is a good time to provide training to the staff who may not have been involved in the scoring process. They will need to know the benefits of having an accurately scored asset criticality, the scoring criteria, how it applies to their work, and how to properly submit corrections. The tool used for scoring can now become a tool for training.

## STEP 7
### Continual Improvement

Criticality is a snapshot of the estimated importance each asset is to an organization at the time it was calculated. As the mission changes,

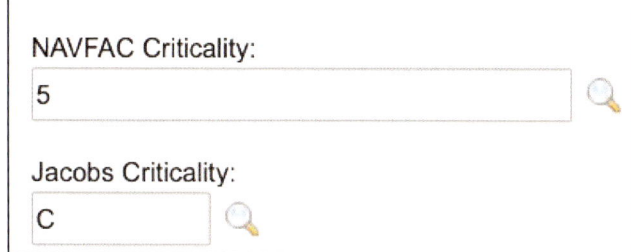

**Figure 5:** An example of two custom fields on an EAM system

technology changes, and even the asset changes, the criticality will no longer be as accurate. How and when the next update should be are dependent on the needs of each organization. Here are some questions to ask to help answer how best to continually improve:

1. How well is the existing criticality being utilized?
2. How much has changed since the analysis?
3. Is the existing criticality being regularly updated?
4. Are new assets being scored as they are installed?
5. What assets do not have a criticality score?

*Mike Castro,* CMRP, CRL, *is a Maintenance and Reliability Engineer for Jacobs Engineering's Asset Management Group. He has over 10 years of experience in facility maintenance, having previously been the M&RE for NASA Goddard Space Flight Center and a Mechanical Engineer for The National Archives before that. He leads the 200+ member Jacobs Asset Management Community of Practice.*

# Join an Uptime® Elements User Group

## Certified Reliability Leaders Advancing the Reliability Framework and Asset Management System

**Uptime Elements Implementation Guide**
Strategy and planning for the annual Uptime® Elements Implementation guide

**Digitalization and IoT**
Working to advance reliability and asset management through digitalization models and IoT

**Sustainability**
Discovering the direct connection between sustainability and reliability

**People and Culture at Work**
Leaning into the inquiry of advancing reliability and asset management through wellness, diversity and inclusion

**Mapping EAM to Uptime Elements**
Using Uptime® Elements as a strategy to supercharge your enterprise asset management system

If you are a Certified Reliability Leader (CRL) please send a message to crm@reliabilityweb.com to discover how to participate.

# MAKING A BUSINESS CASE FOR
# CONDITION-BASED MAINTENANCE

Maciej Kuczyński

It is often said that benefits resulting from mature CBM or implementing PdM include reducing catastrophic events, unplanned outages and routine maintenance costs.

Many are of the opinion that the field of predictive maintenance (PdM) is not growing to its full potential. Among the stated challenges that would need to be effectively addressed before PdM's growth hits the top line, one, in particular, seemed very interesting since it had little to do with technical things. It was a financial justification for condition-based maintenance (CBM) and its more advanced option, in terms of analytics, PdM. Since financial aspects are often overlooked by engineers or not closely examined, this article shares a few thoughts on how to overcome this situation.

It is often said that benefits resulting from mature CBM or implementing PdM include reducing catastrophic events, unplanned outages and routine maintenance costs. Some also mention reducing materials storage together with handling costs. This is all true, but still a little bit vague, incomplete and definitely not enough as a starting point to prepare an appealing business case that would justify spending money on a CBM/PdM project.

First of all, realizing all areas that can benefit from CBM/PdM is crucial for coming up with sound arguments that support a CBM/PdM initiative. Next, it is necessary to understand the mechanisms that actually make the savings happen and, ideally, to evaluate them in terms of finance. This requires more comprehensive analysis and, most importantly, certain business acumen. A shallow approach to this exercise results in leaving out important factors that can lead to false conclusions and underestimating the financial impact and added value of the CBM/PdM project.

At a glance, the ultimate goal of any CBM/PdM project is to optimize operations and maintenance (O&M). Hence, reducing unscheduled downtimes and making a shift to reliability-centered maintenance are among the most recognized deliverables. Therefore, it is hardly surprising that labor and overtime costs, and expedite spending for materials and fleet costs, which correspond to downtimes, are evaluated in depth. This analysis is even more comprehensive since O&M is usually the domain expertise of people directly involved in CBM/PdM projects.

A more challenging area of the O&M analysis is to estimate the value of optimized maintenance resulting from CBM/PdM implementation. This is challenging mainly because of the fact that the prerequisite to accomplishing this task is being aware up-front of the

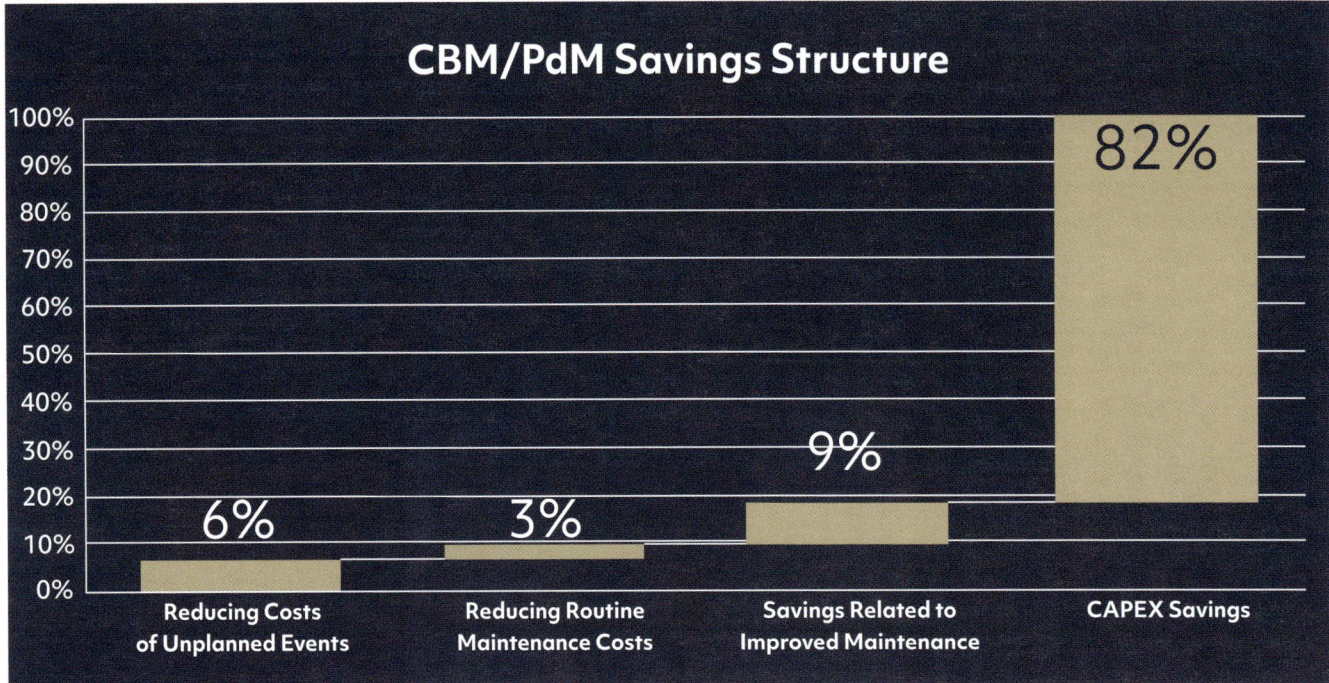

**Figure 1:** An example of savings resulting from CBM/PdM project implementation

business challenges a CBM/PdM solution should address and its expected functionality.

In particular, when dealing with a baseline to optimized maintenance, it is worth taking a closer look at these aspects:

- Decreased maintenance on low-risk assets;
- Maintain high priority, high return on failure (ROF) assets and reduce maintenance on low consequence and low ROF assets;
- Better planning of resources based on assets' performance predictions;
- The optimized scope of maintenance and longer time intervals between routine maintenance;
- Other productivity gains from deploying resources elsewhere.

This lists only a few topics. However, no matter how comprehensive and detailed the O&M study is, identified savings are just the tip of the iceberg. Another savings category is capital expenditures (CapEx). If only evaluated well, CBM/PdM initiatives can reveal their full potential and provide great insight for a business case. The challenge here is that a lot of activities and processes that can be addressed by CBM/PdM are happening behind the scenes from the O&M point of view. Also, people involved in managing CapEx are not necessarily aware of how they could benefit from CBM initiatives. The following points can be considered a baseline for identifying CapEx related savings:

- Capital deferment and depreciation savings by extending the life of existing assets;
- Capital replacement savings by avoiding replacement of the entire piece of equipment;
- Asset replacement strategy based on a risk of failure rather than an age optimized capital spend;
- Capital opportunity costs.

Figure 1 presents an exemplary structure of the possible savings CBM can bring to a power distribution company. It clearly demonstrates how important it is to go beyond classic O&M thinking. What is striking is how CapEx can greatly benefit from projects that are typically linked with O&M.

Depending on the industry and specific business drivers, there are also other aspects that, if assessed, would make good business sense. Even if the task is not straightforward, it is still a good idea to spend some time to at least try to guesstimate savings potential related to:

- Increased reliability and customer satisfaction;
- Increased safety;
- Internal regulatory defense costs;
- A justification for a redeployment of O&M expense budgets;
- Regulatory confidence in risk/cost justification process.

The long-term vision for implementing an asset health strategy is to be in full control of the extent to which a company takes on asset management risk. Because well-defined CBM/PdM is not only about improving maintenance but also managing the operational risk in a cost-effective way, it can help a lot to make this vision a reality.

When considering a CBM/PdM investment, it is definitely advisable to have an in-depth understanding of how an organization can gain leverage from such an initiative. The prerequisite is to have a comprehensive understanding of business drivers and business processes, together with their key performance indicators (KPIs) as a reference point. Knowing this context, it is then possible to identify and quantify improvement possibilities, and prepare a sound business case.

In that regard, having a broad perspective cannot be stressed enough. Bearing in mind that O&M accounts for only a portion of total possible savings, it is important to make sure the group of stakeholders of the CBM/PdM initiative is complete and not limited to O&M representatives.

> **The long-term vision for implementing an asset health strategy is to be in full control of the extent to which a company takes on asset management risk.**

CBM/PdM initiatives that give the same attention to operations, maintenance and business challenges are on the fast track to becoming vital business tools. They can help companies make the most of their assets and create value based on activities that historically used to be a cost center. Additionally, the majority of the organization's added value might be delivered by leveraging relatively simple and well-established techniques that simply provide insight into the assets' health status. So, perhaps some CBM/PdM projects need rethinking and business cases recalculated.

*Maciej Kuczyński* is Global Portfolio Marketing and Sales Manager - Hitachi Energy Grid Integration Services. Maciej has 15 years of engineering and business experience in the industry and infrastructure operational technology area. He specializes in projects related to digital transformation, asset performance management, IIoT/OT security and safety. hitachienergy.com

80 UPTIME

**FEATURED RELIABILITY LEADER**

# PROFESSOR JEZDIMIR KNEZEVIC

**Q. You had a childhood obsession with cars and autosport, progressing to building one by hand and eventually racing that car. How did your car racing get you started on your study of reliability?**

**A.** The objective of racing is to be first, but to be first, first you have to finish. So, not finishing was caused by failures of the car, some of which could have been rectified with allowed 30 minute delays, which means you had to have adequate spare parts, tools and equipment to do the repair. Hence, during the two years of rallying, I was looking for the answer to the question, "At the beginning of each rally, should I take a new water, oil, or petrol pump as a spare or get all three secondhand? As I could not find any body of knowledge to help me with the answer, I decided to study reliability, which seemed the best subject available.

**Q. Did you think you would be drawn into engineering and maintenance?**

**A.** Well, I expected that studies of reliability would cover maintenance, but they did not. So, after obtaining a Master's Degree in Reliability Engineering and completing my PhD studies in Maintenance Engineering – which from the theoretical point of view are very different from reliability – I became a mechanical engineer with postgraduate degrees in reliability and maintenance, but still actively seeking the answers to my "crossing the finish line" questions. That journey brought me to many universities and scientific organizations worldwide, each of which gave a part of the answer, but I was still looking for a coherent and comprehensive body of knowledge that would address my rallying concerns.

**Q. When you established the Centre for Management of Industrial Reliability, Cost and Effectiveness (MIRCE) at Exeter University, UK, what did you envision it would become?**

**A.** My main aim was to create an academic environment that would focus on building a scientific bridge between reliability and maintenance, which, in my view, are essential for the cost-effective operation of industrial systems. Through MIRCE, I started teaching reliability and maintenance courses to undergraduate students of engineering science (e.g., mechanical, electrical, civil and chemical), which was the first in the UK. Within the Centre, we have an Industrial Club, consisting of around 2,500 members, like design engineers, maintainers, logisticians, racing drivers, pilots, mathematicians, physicists, business managers, psychologists, meteorologists and many other professions that have an impact on "crossing the finish line" in my case of delivering business plans with private and governmental originations. I am proud to emphasize that the existence of the Centre was based exclusively on the earnings generated by our teaching, training and consulting activities, which means that during the 13 years of existence, we have not spent a single amount of taxpayers' money, which is not that common for university communities.

**Q. Describe the various master's programs you have developed?**

**A.** MIRCE offered the first European master's degree programs in reliability and maintainability engineering, logistics engineering, and system operational effectiveness. These courses were designed for people from industry with a minimum of five years of experience who needed to introduce operational reality into their office full of mechanical, electrical, civil and aeronautical engineers with no in-service experience. These are exactly the type of people I would have become had I not had rallying and racing experience. These part-time degree programs were supported by the global giants, like British Aerospace, Lockheed, Rolls-Royce, Siemens, Dowty Shorts, Bombardier, Westland Helicopters, the Royal Air Force, the South African Navy, the NATO Maintenance and Supply Agency (NAMSA), Martin-Baker, Lucas Aerospace, United Defense, GES Avionics, and many other companies worldwide. To deliver such complex programs, we had 23 professors from seven different departments within Exeter University and numerous guest lecturers from aerospace, defense, nuclear power and other industries worldwide.

**Q. Describe in layman's terms what MIRCE Science is?**

**A.** After 10 years of running postgraduate programs, over 200 students met Exeter University's requirements for a Master's degree. However, I realized that we still did not have a coherent body of knowledge to provide a scientific answer to my "crossing the finish line" reliability and maintenance questions. To fully focus on my scientific endeavor, I resigned from Exeter University in 1999, which closed the MIRCE as there was nobody to run it, and established the MIRCE Akademy at Woodbury Park, that time owned by Nigel Mansell, the 1992 Formula One and 1993 IndyCar World Champion. During the following 10 years, together with students, members and fellows of the Akademy, a new body of scientific knowledge was created that I named MIRCE Science. It provides quantitative answers to the questions I was posing during my rallying time 30 years ago through a system of equations, rules and methods that explain and predict measurable performance of future functionable systems, and minimizes occurrences of "nasty surprises," both physical and monetary, during their in-service lives at a time when the changes require minimum time, money and energy. The simplest example is: If for the same investment it is possible to double reliability or half maintenance, which option should be taken and why?

**Q. Do you have an industrial example of the value add from applying MIRCE Science?**

**A.** MIRCE Science has been the foundation of the creation of training and procedures activities during the establishment of the Airbus Operability Department. It was used during the designs of the A380 and A350 passenger aircraft through training courses run at Filton, UK; Toulouse, France; Bremen, Germany; and Madrid, Spain. Also, MIRCE Science was a foundation for getting and delivering various research projects, like these:

- Development of operability laws, Airbus, Toulouse, France;
- Review of Airbus A380 operational reliability prediction model and its results in relation to in-service data, Airbus, Toulouse, France;
- Development of enhanced failure data analysis techniques for improved aircraft reliability performance, Airbus, Toulouse, France;
- Identification of prediction and assessment technique for aircraft operability, Airbus, Toulouse, France;
- Human error analysis in maintenance, Airbus, Filton, UK.

The results of our research have been firmly embedded into Airbus and approved and used in processes and procedures and the equivalent documents for thousands of their suppliers worldwide.

**Q. As a student of MIRCE, what opportunities are provided? Are there particular organizations where your students can apply what they have learned?**

**A.** Our students are exposed to the new way of addressing and understanding in-service behavior of functionable systems. For example, currently used reliability block diagrams of an aircraft do not contain a single block related to air, which is essential for both functionality and functionability of it. So, our students are the new type of top decision makers who are able to foresee the future of in-service performance of the products and services at the time when the most significant decisions and trade-offs are made among competing options and the consequences that will be faced by users, operators, humans and the environment during several decades and centuries. Hence, our students are "responsible" for all reliability and maintenance design-in characteristics that unquestionably drive in-service performance, cost and the safety of nuclear submarines, space stations, spacecrafts, power stations, industrial plants, military systems, and the like. In fact, many of them do not even know yet that this type of expert even exists! Obvious candidates are SpaceX, NASA, Virgin Galactic, the European Space Agency (ESA) and similar organizations that are dealing with projects for which in-service data does not exist at all and yet the projects must proceed!

**Q. During one of your presentations at The RELIABILITY Conference 2019, you mentioned the Monte Carlo simulation. This was a bit of a breakthrough for you. Can you elaborate why that was?**

**A.** I conceived the mathematical system of equations required for the applications of MIRCE Science about 15 years ago, but their complexity was beyond the ability of mathematical methods to generate the numerical results. However, that was not only a problem of MIRCE Science, but all scientific disciplines that are based on an infinite sum of convolution integrals. Faced with that problem, developers of nuclear bombs at the Los Alamos National Laboratory in New Mexico developed an alternative method for solving those integrals under the code name "Monte Carlo." Hence, when I, educated as a deterministic mechanical engineer, learned about it from my dear colleague and friend, the late Professor Arie Dubi, a Grand Fellow of MIRCE Akademy, the door for the applications of MIRCE Science fully opened. By making use of the Monte Carlo simulation, it became possible to predict the expected functionability performance of systems, the complexity of which is governed by multi-dimensional relationships of thousands of consisting components that are exposed to aging processes, maintenance induced errors, environmental conditions during operation, transportation and storage, and complicated regulations and rules, all of which are properly defined and incorporated into MIRCE functionability, maintainability, supportability, operability and profitability equations.

**Q. You have written three books. Who is your target audience? Do you need to be a mathematician to read and understand them?**

**A.** The books that I authored or coauthored are addressed to practicing engineers, managers, students and researchers. As mathematics is the only human activity that enables predictions to be made by using a necessary equation, a working knowledge of mathematics is required, which is far from being a mathematician! MIRCE Science equations could be successfully incorporated into software, which drastically reduces demands for complex mathematical calculations. For that reason, the practical applications of the Monte Carlo simulations were only possible with a development of modern computers.

**Q. What's next for you? Your work?**

**A.** Great question! The theoretical part of MIRCE Science is completed, tested and verified. However, my greatest challenge for the future is twofold:

- First, continuous research toward the understanding of physical mechanisms that govern occurrences of functionability events within the scale of $10^{-10}$ of a meter (atomic scale) and $10^{+10}$ of a meter (solar system), which is necessary for the accuracy of the predictions;
- Second, finding the best media for transferring a half of century of my experience and passion for generating the body of knowledge for increasing probability of "crossing the finish line" with new generations of scientists, engineers, managers and, above all, technologists, who are needed for the development of the software that would enable easier applications of MIRCE functionability equations and "taming" the artificial intelligence community to focus also on the generation of the future data rather than to analyze the past one.

**Q. You often mention the word functionability. What is the difference between functionality and functionability as far as MIRCE Science is concerned?**

**A.** Thank you for paying attention to my statements. Functionally is related to inherent properties and performance of an asset, product, or service. For example, a functionality of a commercial aircraft is described through measures like speed, range, carrying capacity, fuel consumption, etc. However, the functionability performance of the same aircraft is related to its in-service punctuality, number of maintenance man-hours, crew commonality, logistics delay times, and similar measures experienced by operators and users. For example, the very first B747, flown by Pan Am, had been airborne 80,000 hours in revenue generating services, but it had been exposed to 806,000 maintenance man-hours, over 22 years of its life span. In summary, well established sciences like thermodynamics, material science, fluid mechanics, electrodynamics and similar deal with functionality performance, whereas MIRCE Science, to the best of my knowledge, is the only one that deals with functionability performance.

# AMP
Association of Asset Management Professionals

## The Association of Asset Management Professionals

**> AIM:** Creating awareness, demand and knowledge around asset management.

**> Mission:** To provide professional accreditation and acknowkledgment in learning, advancement opportunities, and career development in asset management.

**> Vision:** To be a respectful, diverse and global community for professionals to exchange ideas and to advance asset management.

## Certifications

AMP Currently offers certifications for reliability and asset management professionals.

Certified Reliability Leader     Certified Maintenance Leader

Both certifications align with the ISO/IEC 17024, wich is the standard developed for the objective of achieving and promoting a globally accepted benchmark for organizations operating certification of persons.

## Join for Free!
www.AssetManagementProfessionals.org

# Earn a Domain Mastery Belt!

The CRL Domain Mastery Belt Program is a results-oriented acknowledgment of significant and successful holistic reliability improvement projects delivered on a consistent basis.

## Mastery Domains:

- AM Yellow Belt – Asset Management
- REM Orange Belt – Reliability Engineering for Maintenance
- ACM Green Belt – Asset Condition Management
- WEM Blue Belt – Work Execution Management
- LER Red Belt – Leadership for Reliability
- CRL Black Belt - Complete all Domains

## Learn More:
AssetManagementProfessionals.Org/Certification

# the Stand
## Hosted by Terrence O'Hanlon

**INNOVATIONS** HIGH-LEVEL STRATEGY  **EMERGING TRENDS** IN ASSET MANAGEMENT

### SPECIAL GUEST
### Advergus Taylor

Advergus has been treating wastewater for over 34 years for Clark County Water Reclamation District in Southern Nevada, east of the Las Vegas Strip. His career there started at age 14 as a summer job, advancing to full-time, all the way to his current position as the Plant Operations Manager and Process Control of the water treatment facility.

Advergus was exposed to reliability back in 2013 when he attended the The International Maintenance Conference (IMC). What he learned from attending the IMC had a profound effect on him, how reliability can play a major role in the operation & maintenance of his wastewater facility.

He wrote a post trip report to his leadership team about the conference and how their organization should tap into the world of reliability.

He involved more coworkers by bringing them to conferences and sharing articles about reliability and its value. Once his peers were exposed to the reliability culture, they started to see and speak the same language.

The reliability journey has been long, but according to Advergus, it's well worth it.

---

Reliabilityweb.com CEO and *Uptime*® bookazine Publisher Terrence O'Hanlon sat down with Advergus as a guest on "The Stand," available as an on-demand video; the interview transcript is below.

**Terrence O'Hanlon:** If you were going to use the Uptime® Elements A Reliability Framework and Asset Management System to describe your current activities, what would you say?

**Advergus Taylor:** Right now, we are focusing on the orange domain, which represents Reliability Engineering for Maintenance. We just finished a huge plant expansion design and we incorporated RCD (reliability-centered design).

**TO:** That's great!

**AT:** We actually auditioned five different RCD facilitators to be part of that project.

**TO:** That's fantastic, sort of knocking that maintenance mountain down to a maintenance molehill. Were there any innovations you can tell us about? A lot of teams try reliability-centered design, but they don't always get warm welcomes or send the most experienced people to the meetings. What can you tell us about any success factors or innovations you discovered during that process?

**AT:** We made sure that some of the best certified reliability leaders on our internal staff participated. We had several CRLs from our plant operation staff and maintenance staff plan and schedule to be part of the project review meetings to represent asset management and reliability. It was different because everybody participates and facilitates reliability-centered design just a little bit differently. We are trying

**DYNAMIC** CONVERSATION   **BIG IDEAS** FROM EXPERTS   **POWERFUL** INSIGHTS

to find that sweet spot where I would say probably 80% of the team was aligned with the reliability goals.

The reliability journey is long, but it's well worth it.

**TO:** Did you manage to keep it on budget and on schedule? Did your team have to make any major design changes?

**AT:** We did change a few things, but those changes came from onetime opportunities.

From our perspective, it's more about the total cost of ownership over the entire asset lifecycle. Putting the work in now avoids the "pay me now or pay me later" syndrome. We want to pay now because the savings come from doing it now. If you go back and do it later on…

**TO:** So, what are you dealing with right now?

**AT:** Currently, we're facing long lead times on equipment and parts.

**TO:** So, the team probably appreciates reliability-centered design now?

**AT:** It took a little while, but they did because it was something new for engineering. Hopefully, we can keep doing it so we can continuously improve.

**TO:** What was the outcome? Did the start-up go well?

**AT:** One of the projects is starting right now. At this point, concrete is being poured.

**TO:** What kind of advice would you give to people who might be interested in integrating reliability-centered design?

**AT:** The benefit of doing RCD up-front is not just from a cost perspective, but also to enhance the team's asset knowledge.

Our team was pleased. Some had a little push and pull with our engineering, but overall we collaborated well cross-functionally.

**TO:** Do you think you'll continue with the RCD program as you do future capital projects and expansions?

**AT:** Yes, we are going to put the reliability and asset management effort into the process up-front rather than going back and trying to do Reliability Strategy Design [RSD] after start-up.

**TO:** Any other advice for the reliability leader community that is reading this?

**AT:** Don't stop the journey. That means just keep going. Baby steps, you know, those baby steps. Don't stop. Keep going. Keep going.

**TO:** I think it's great advice and it matches Winston Churchill's famous quote "If you're going through hell, keep going."

**Thank you very much for joining us, Advergus. You are a true reliability leader.**

Many industry experts report that most failures (i.e., defects) during an asset's operational phase are the result of poor or inadequate design. Many times, design omissions are caused by insufficient funds or budget constraints imposed due to a lack of understanding of the consequences on the lifecycle costs of the asset.

AUGUST 2023   89

# SKILLS IN DEMAND

Source: The Most In-Demand Skills for Reliability and Asset Management Survey by Reliabilityweb.com

## How would you describe yourself using these descriptions?

The top 35% of participants are more likely to work at corporate for multiple plants as the highest prevalence of work descriptions.

- 23% — I work in a single location plant
- 12% — I work in multiple location plants
- 35% — I work at corporate for multiple plants
- 30% — I am a solution provider or consultant

## How would you rate the maturity of your organization's reliability and asset management journey?

Organizations with reactive planned are considered to be more reliable in the organization's asset management.

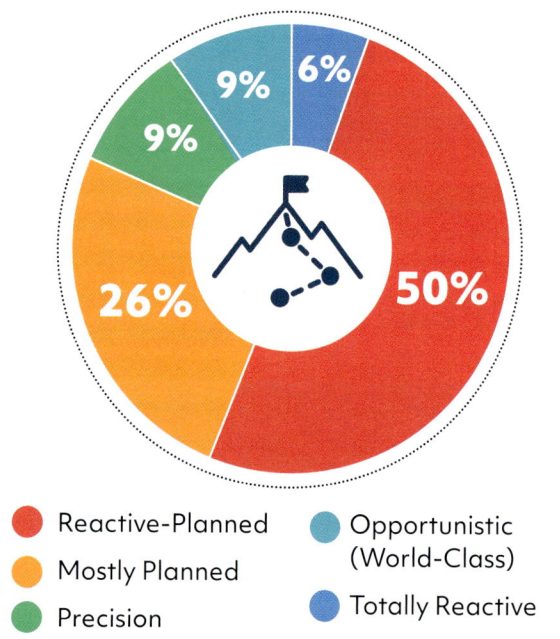

- 50% Reactive-Planned
- 26% Mostly Planned
- 9% Precision
- 9% Opportunistic (World-Class)
- 6% Totally Reactive

## What are the top 10 in demand skills by vote across all domains?

The top three in-demand skills observed from all the domain records are Lubrication and Contamination Control, Root Cause, and Computerized Maintenance Management System.

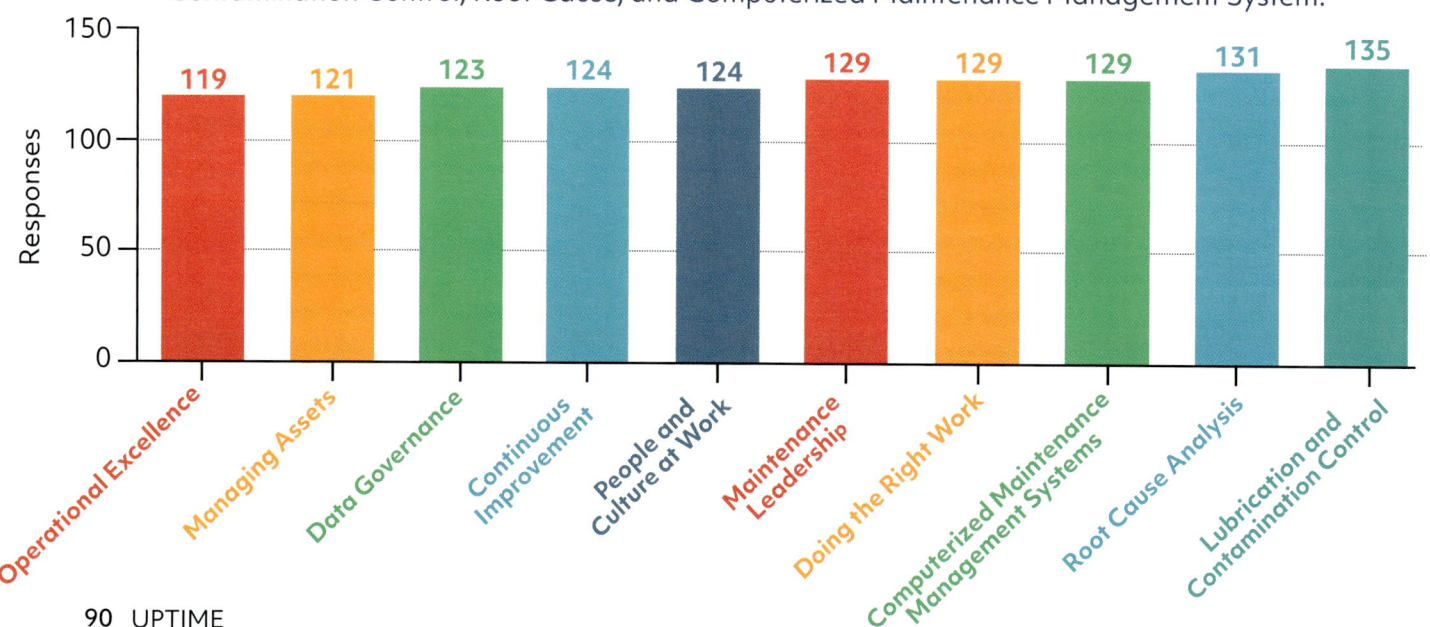

| Skill | Responses |
|---|---|
| Operational Excellence | 119 |
| Managing Assets | 121 |
| Data Governance | 123 |
| Continuous Improvement | 124 |
| People and Culture at Work | 124 |
| Maintenance Leadership | 129 |
| Doing the Right Work | 129 |
| Computerized Maintenance Management Systems | 129 |
| Root Cause Analysis | 131 |
| Lubrication and Contamination Control | 135 |

## Which geographic region best describes the location you work from?

A large number of participants belong to the USA (48%) as a working location.

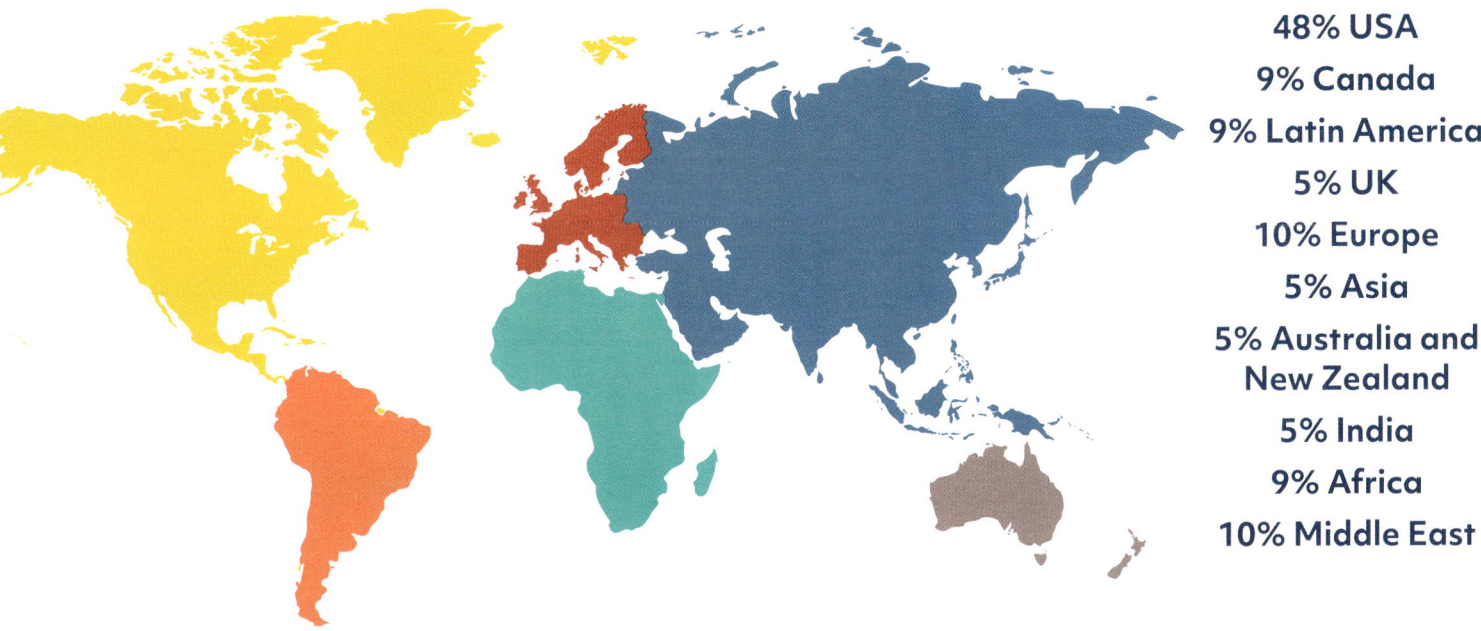

48% USA
9% Canada
9% Latin America
5% UK
10% Europe
5% Asia
5% Australia and New Zealand
5% India
9% Africa
10% Middle East

## Who is directly responsible for competency-based learning and skills development for reliability and asset management in your organization?

The plant maintenance manager is most likely to hold these responsibilities at survey participants' organizations.

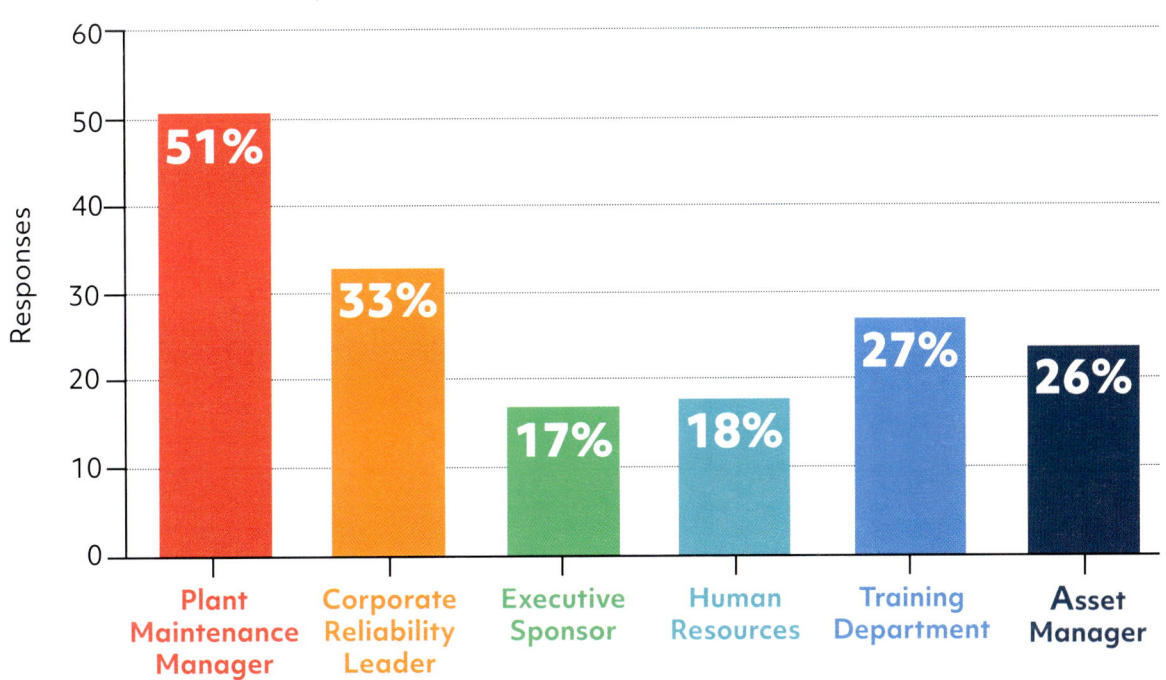

AUGUST 2023

# Maximize asset value, improve safety and boost productivity.

Discover why IFS is
#1 in Enterprise Asset
Management software.

ifs.com

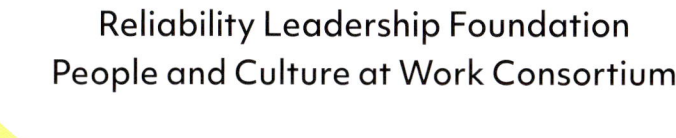
Reliability Leadership Foundation
People and Culture at Work Consortium

# BREAKING THE BARRIERS IN RELIABILITY

A Report on How Attention to Diversity, Equity, and Inclusion Changes Your Reliability Results

## A dedicated team from the People and Culture at Work Consortium created this important report:

Melissa Ruth
Sean Mullan
Joseph Uwoajega
Maura Abad
Gabriela Mejias

## Additional People and Culture at Work Consortium members who support the outcomes include:

Monique Mirabeau
Lauren Wilder
Laura Goebel
David Ruth
Paddy Douglas
Rhonda Bullard
Yamina Palma

# Introduction

## Why I Should Care

Diversity is a word that seems to either bring out the fanatics or cause people to run away. Yet, it is an aspect that must be addressed in everything we do. Multiple published reports show that the world generally benefits when diversity is embraced. As we will discuss later in more detail, the reports do not directly address the reliability and maintenance world. There are many missing aspects to how diversity and inclusion can be identified, tracked, and embraced.

The current and future reliability and maintenance community labor situation is very concerning. We've all had conversations about where we will find talent as our experienced employees retire. We've experienced the skills gaps before. Now, in this post-pandemic world, we find ourselves in an even tougher situation—a full-on labor gap. If we don't act now, this labor shortage will continue to negatively affect our industry and world.

As you read through this document, consider this: Your employees are a significant part of the company's intellectual property (IP). All teams are either assets or liabilities. While a team may be an asset now, it can quickly become a liability if they are not prepared. Consider what a difference your team would make if you saw increased innovation, improved productivity, supply chain improvements, and reputation improvement across the board. These are all benefits other companies have seen by embracing diversity, inclusion, equity, and belonging in everything they do. The goal of this report is to show how embracing diversity will enhance that asset in new ways.

## Terminology

The People and Culture at Work Consortium recently published a glossary (see QR code below) with terms and more. That and more can be found at Reliabilityweb.com. While all the terms below are also in the glossary, we want to take a few moments to review terms that apply directly to this report. They are diversity, equity, inclusion, and belonging (DEIB). Note that an entire report could be written for each term. In this report, however, we want to focus on how they work together for your teams.

- **Diversity (as per Reliabilityweb.com):**
  Diversity is a variety of uniqueness, difference of view, perception, ideas, and approaches that result in value creation for the organization through inclusion to advance reliability and asset management.

- **Equity**
  The policy or practice of accounting for the differences in each individual's starting point when pursuing a goal or achievement, and working to remove barriers to equal opportunity, as by providing support based on the unique needs of individual students or employees.

- **Inclusion**
  Inclusion is an active, intentional, and continuous process to address inequities in power and privilege and build a respectful and diverse

**Glossary with Terms**
Scan code or visit website

http://uptime4.me/Diversity-Inclusion-Glossary

community that ensures welcoming spaces and opportunities to flourish for all.

- **Belonging**
  Belonging is the feeling of security and support when there is a sense of acceptance, inclusion, and identity for a member of a certain group. It is when an individual can bring their authentic self to work. When employees feel like they don't belong at work, their performance and their personal lives suffer. Creating genuine feelings of belonging for all is a critical factor in improving engagement and performance. It also helps support business goals. People need to feel valued.

While each of these terms is important on its own, it's important to understand how much stronger they are when they work together. As more studies have been completed, the terms have grown and evolved. Initially, we heard the word diversity and assumed we knew what that meant without any study. Diversity is more than just what can be seen. It is more than just acknowledging what makes us different. Seeing and acknowledging obvious differences can hurt the goal of having a cohesive team. As seen in the diagram below, it is critical that we embrace the idea that diversity is just one aspect of a diversity initiative.

When putting things into action, think of diversity as being invited to the party without having to ask for an invite. Think of inclusion as having the music to dance and not being judged for your moves. Think of equity as being able to attend the dance without any barriers or access issues. Lastly, as this diagram shows, belonging is the perfect combination of all three.

# State of the Workforce

## U.S. Bureau of Labor Statistics

The U.S. Department of Labor Bureau of Labor Statistics (BLS) has been capturing data about the workforce for decades. One can evaluate the data from multiple perspectives—age, race, gender, education received, and more.

One data graph provided by the BLS indicates that out of the 614,000 total employed in maintenance in 2021, only 5,100 were women. When looking at the race statistics, we can see another large discrepancy. Black or African American, Asian, and Hispanic make up less than half (32.3 percent) of maintenance and repair workers category, while the remaining are White (84.6).

Another concern is age. The age of the available and trained workforce is getting older. When looking at the statistics from an age perspective, we can see that the median age for all maintenance related jobs is 42.9. However, the industry has 1,165,000 employees that will age out of the

system. There are only 496,000 employees in the workforce under 24. These numbers will lead to an eventual issue where we have more work than we have employees. This is complicated by the fact that the industry gets more technical every day, and employees who can handle the technical aspects of the job are needed. Remember that the latest data available from the BLS is from 2021. Many maintenance and reliability departments have already begun struggling with a shortage of

| Household Data: Annual Averages | | | | | | |
|---|---|---|---|---|---|---|
| Employed persons by detailed occupation, sex, race, and Hispanic or Latino ethnicity (Numbers in thousands) | | | | | | |
| | 2021 | | | | | |
| Occupation | Total Employed | Women | White | Black or African American | Asian | Hispanic or Latino |
| Total, 16 years and over | 152,581 | 47% | 77.5% | 12.3% | 6.6% | 18% |
| Maintenance and repair workers, general | 614 | 5.1% | 84.6% | 8.8% | 2.5% | 21% |

**Figure 1:** Source U.S. Bureau of Labor Statistics https://www.bls.gov/cps/cpsaat11.htm

## BREAKING THE BARRIERS IN RELIABILITY

available workers. With the data we have, we have an employee shortage crisis coming very soon.

These statistics clearly show that the maintenance and reliability industry is not diverse in terms of race, gender, and age. However, that is not the full story.

## What's Missing?

### Maintenance and Reliability Specifics

Data specific to maintenance and reliability is difficult to find. The BLS pulls information from the U.S. Census and attempts to pool this data by occupation. While representative, some maintenance technicians may self-report their occupation as "millwright" or "electrician." They would, therefore, be excluded from the "maintenance" fields in Figure 1. Nonetheless, the trend in these fields is as the data shows.

While there are many studies that point to the many benefits of diversity in teams, these studies were focused on upper management, administrative, or software teams. These have not focused on maintenance or reliability departments.

### Global Statistics

Finding global statistics directly related to maintenance and reliability has also been challenging. The Organization for Economic Co-operation and Development (OECD.org) has done some work to help define barriers to stable employment that includes issues such as age and (dis)ability. It is unclear if the OECD has considered other diversity issues. It is important to note the aspects that make up diversity look different in different regions around the world. Each region is affected not only by education requirements, but also the availability of education and training, access, gender, race, and much more. ■

| | **Household Data: Annual Averages** Employed persons by detailed occupation and age (Numbers in thousands) | | | | | | | | |
|---|---|---|---|---|---|---|---|---|---|
| | **2021** | | | | | | | | |
| **Occupation** | Total, 16 Years and Over | 16-19 Years | 20-24 Years | 25-34 Years | 35-44 Years | 45-54 Years | 55-64 Years | 65 Years and Over | Median Age |
| Total Employed | 152,581 | 5,266 | 13,409 | 34,578 | 32,734 | 30,554 | 25,912 | 10,127 | 42.2% |
| Installation, maintenance, and repair occupations | 4,840 | 100 | 396 | 1,120 | 1,039 | 1,021 | 900 | 265 | 42.9% |

**Figure 2:** Source U.S. Bureau of Labor Statistics https://www.bls.gov/cps/cpsaat11b.htm

# Aspects of DEIB

As reliability leaders, we deal not only with assets, but also with people. Understanding diversity will help us better lead change, inspire creativity, and implement action. Diversity comes in many forms, but generally there are four types of workplace diversity.

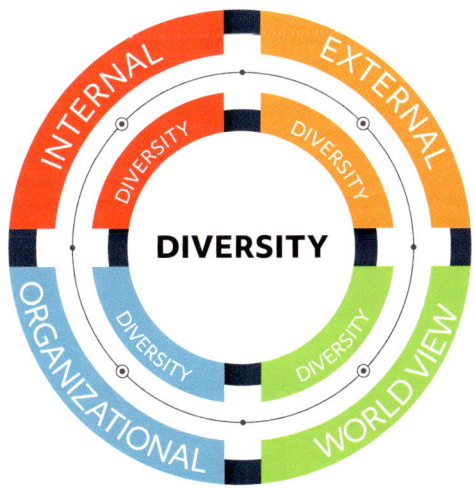

## Internal Diversity

There are certain inherited traits we are born into. We cannot change these aspects. Often, when we think of diversity, our tendency is to think of these characteristics first.

## External Diversity

As we grow and move into adulthood, outside factors and opportunities define our personalities and make us unique. External diversity considers the events that shape us into who we are. A person's location, family status, and socio-economic status could also be considered factors of external diversity.

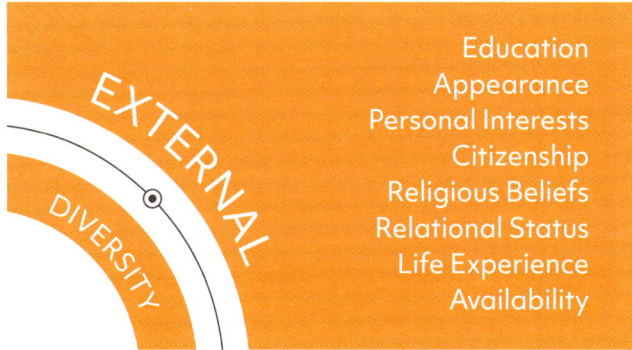

## Worldview Diversity

Everyone has different life experiences and these events and encounters are unique to each of us. Shared events may impact people differently based on other diverse traits and how we perceive the event. Some members of a group may not have faced the same situation and cannot share in the experience. Worldview diversity encompasses how our past experiences and life events

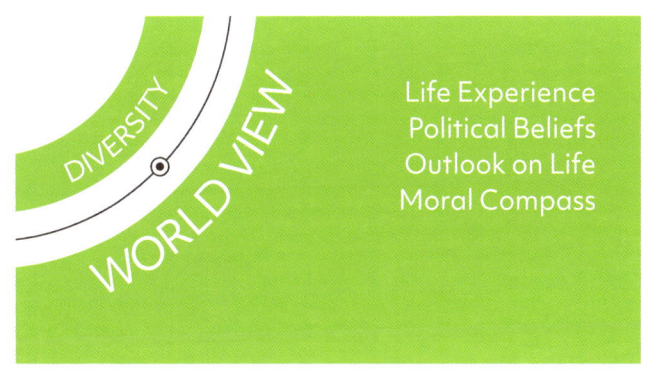

## BREAKING THE BARRIERS IN RELIABILITY

have shaped our personalities. It is important to note that worldview diversity characteristics may change with time and experience.

## Functional or Organizational Diversity

Every group we belong to has a structure of varying degrees, written rules and unwritten rules that define the group. Social and work groups have unique structures that create diversity due to the way members of the group are organized. This is called functional or organizational diversity.

## Summary

Embracing diversity is more than identifying the type of diversity and the nuances that come with it. We must understand that each type of diversity is individual. Each type is uniquely complex and is often not a singular aspect our colleagues experience. In fact, understanding the overlap of many attributes will likely change how we holistically track and manage diversity programs.

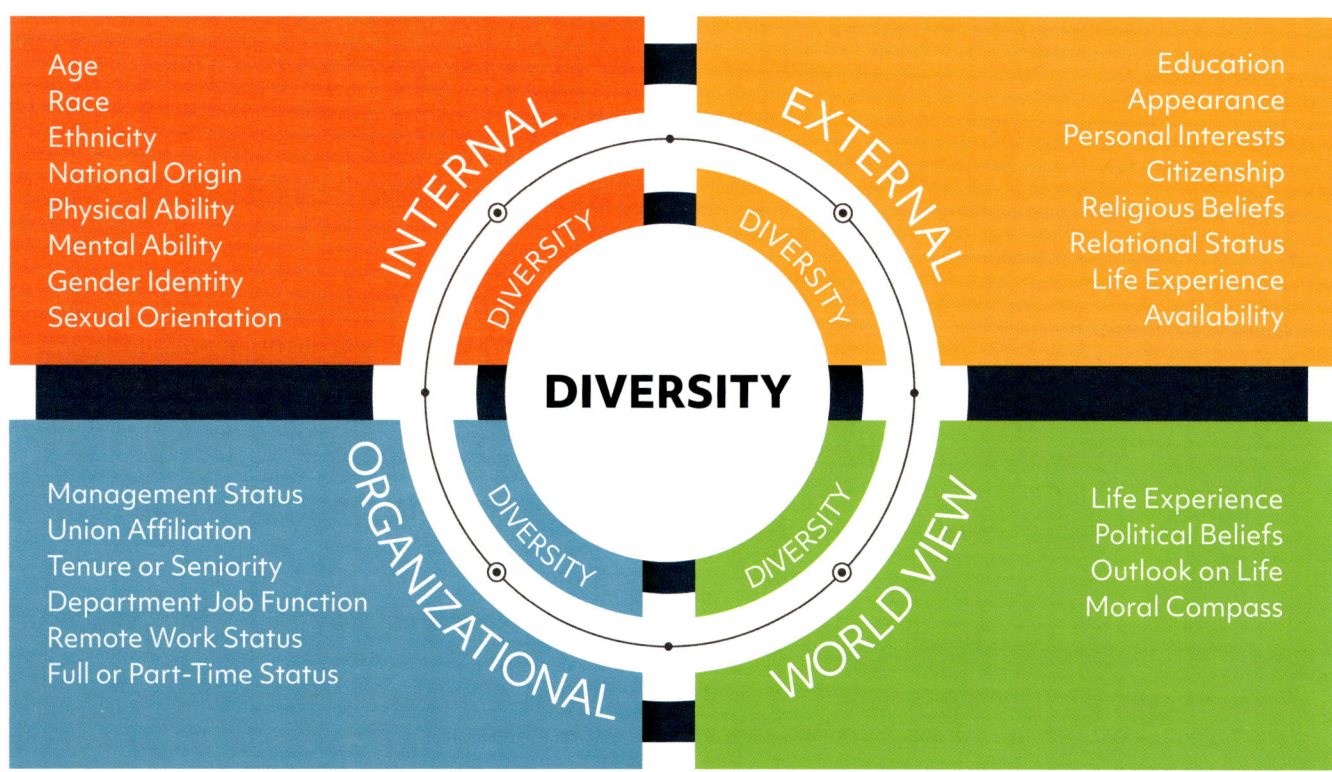

# How Will Paying Attention to DEIB Change My Results?

Through this document, we have learned about the different types of diversity and the importance and impact of diversity, equity, inclusion, and belonging. How does this all tie into reliability and asset management? How does embracing DEIB improve our results, and where are the links to the Uptime Elements framework?

The Leadership for Reliability (LER) domain elements deal with the culture of reliability in an organization. Strategy alone is not sustainable. It takes leadership and culture to establish a mindset and culture in an organization. This is the most important domain's for ensuring efforts employed to achieve the organization's aim are met. The LER domain's focus is also to drive continuous improvement to ensure efforts are supported and sustained.

As we have outlined, a more diverse group brings new perspectives, viewpoints, and experiences to a group. Engaging and ensuring that everyone's voice is heard and considered leads us to finding the best course of action to achieve the group's mission or aim. It is the collective intellect that will drive culture.

> **It takes leadership and culture to establish a mindset and culture in an organization.**

Tactically speaking, specific elements from the framework also are highly impacted by DEIB.

Diversity brings new perspectives to problem-solving. Root cause analysis (RCA) results will be stronger with a diverse group that is engaged. When RCA is ingrained in an organization's continuous improvement culture, improvement is more effective and sustainable. Decision-making improves with diversity as the team will have a broader understanding of the balance of cost, risk, and value.

Lastly, let's consider the element of corporate responsibility. Corporate responsibility defines how the organization will manage the impact of the organization on the community and the environment. This element is relevant to asset management because it helps drive decision-making. Organizations have an impact on the communities they operate in. Those communities include financial, economic, environmental, and social.

Diversity, equity, inclusion, and belonging are drivers of culture. A culture of reliability will help us achieve success in the triple bottom line of people, profit, and planet.

# Barriers

There are many barriers to adopting a culture that truly embraces diversity, equity, inclusion, and belonging. These barriers are not always identified and, if not identified, can block the effectiveness of any program. We share these with you not to overwhelm you, but to help you ensure you understand the barriers. For each barrier, we will also identify ways to address and overcome them. Note that these barriers are not listed in any specific priority order.

## Vocabulary Comprehension

Diversity, equity, inclusion, and belonging are terms that are used in a plethora of situations. The meaning of these words, however, can be altered by the perception and knowledge of the listener. Misunderstanding the terms can lead to a misunderstanding of the meaning behind agendas pushed out. In that case, the culture of inclusion and belonging will fail to be created.

**Ways to Counteract This Barrier:**

Ensure that everyone understands the four terms. This will ensure that the spirit behind the message is portrayed correctly. To ease that endeavor, the consortium has published a helpful glossary that you may use.

## Bias

Just as perceptions drive an employee's understanding of DEIB, so too will their inherent biases. As is defined in the glossary, inherent bias is often unknown to the individual and will require some awareness about what inherent bias is and how they can find which ones play a role in their lives. In fact, it is also known as unconscious bias.

One interesting aspect is that unconscious or inherent bias is usually determined by a person's upbringing, experiences, and local culture. Therefore, you will find that the same inherent bias issues do not exist at each facility around the country. In one area, there may be an inherent bias against people of a specific race, but you may not see that in other facilities that are physically located elsewhere.

**Ways to Counteract This Barrier:**

Knowledge is the first step to change. Sharing with colleagues about what implicit bias is, as well as how it affects them, will go a long way to ensure people start holding themselves accountable for their own implicit biases. There are two tools that can assist you on this endeavor.

1. An Introduction to the Implicit Association Test (IAT)[1] is a video published by Olson Zaltman. You can refer to it and use it to assist you in counteracting this barrier. It's short and can be included in any presentation shared with your employees.

2. Project Implicit[2] has done a good amount of research on implicit bias through Harvard University. It has put together several assessments to help others determine what their own implicit biases are. The Harvard Implicit Association Test[3] is an easy way for an individual to identify their own unconscious biases and begin to learn that they actually exist.

Knowledge is the first step to true change. Incorporating these links after showing the video can allow your own employees to self-identify and start course correcting.

## Be Cautionary of Labels

One of the most common trackers for DEIB used across the USA is tracking labels. Around the country, there are multiple awards a company can win based on their growth in the diversity sector. These awards often track demographics to determine just "how diverse" a company is and its progress. The struggle here is that diversity and inclusion are more than what you can see or identify in that way. It's a large part of the culture. While someone with a race that isn't White may appear to be diverse because of their label, it's important to acknowledge that we are not diverse when we are with people who match our demographics. For example, a White person on a board of all Black people could be considered diverse. Likewise, a male on a board that is otherwise all females could be considered as diverse.

To complicate matters, the description of diversity provided by Reliabilityweb.com's diversity hackathon points to differences in job titles, experience, education, and decision-making processing. Therefore, the consortium recommends that while tracking numbers can assist and show you how you are progressing, you should consider labels in context. Let HR focus on the demographics.

**Ways to Counteract This Barrier:**

Instead of looking at labels, take an honest look at your departments, your teams, and your project teams. Let's call these working groups for this explanation. When looking at these, consider the following in addition to the demographics:

- Are they effective at thinking outside of the box?
- Are we getting the best results possible?

- Does this working group have healthy debate about how to address issues or are they all agreeing with the person who appears to be the leader?
- Is there any aspect of performing?
- Are they all from the same department?
- Do they have the same education level?
- Is there any variation in personality styles within this working group?
- Is there diversity of thought in the group?
- Is everyone being heard?

These kinds of questions allow you to see how working groups are working and if they are working to their best potential. Otherwise, it's possible that you are missing a few key diversity aspects.

## Decision-Making Processes & Procedures

It is important to assess existing procedures for implicit bias. Take time to understand the history of existing processes to uncover any root biases. This includes evaluating recruiting and hiring processes with an open mind. However, there are a few potential barriers to this:

1. Current processes and procedures often were created out of historical experience, unknowingly including existing implicit biases.
2. There may be significant emotional attachment to existing processes or procedures by existing employees.
3. It can be a big endeavor to evaluate existing processes and procedures.

**Ways to Counteract This Barrier:**

Create a diverse team to evaluate existing procedures with the following guidelines:

1. Create a list of all existing processes or procedures.
2. Prioritize a review of existing procedures or processes based on the potential impact in affecting diversity and inclusion within your company. Note that the review includes meeting with those who currently use those existing procedures and processes.
3. Evaluate processes and procedures based on the priority list with an open mind. Then provide a list of recommendations to upper management.

## Checking the Box

A cursory review of most of the well-known diversity programs and companies who win diversity awards will lead you to realize that existing programs largely focus on checking boxes. This has led to companies reporting on how many people of diverse characteristics have been hired, are on the board, are in management, or how many have been promoted. While this is a convenient way of tracking "success," this doesn't necessarily indicate a thriving diverse workplace or culture. Meeting number requirements doesn't always mean that a healthy culture is being adopted within the facility, or how effective those efforts have been. In addition, aspects of diversity can only be considered diversity based on the group they are around. For example, a group of people with the same skin color may or may not be diverse.

**Ways to Counteract This Barrier:**

Identify diversity agendas that are focused not on numbers from a high level, but on individual departments. The major aspects of diversity are already known by human resources.

Identify belonging and inclusion agendas that are focused either on campus or department. True diversity involves equity and inclusion as a result. It is more than what you can see and it is not easily tracked. ■

# How to Leverage Diversity Initiatives to Improve Your Reliability

## Take a Stand and Make Diversity a Priority

Making diversity a priority is not just about following HR rules. There's a need for everyone to make it a priority. It's up to you and your working groups to make diversity a priority every day.

This is important because each employee has their own viewpoint about inclusion. You can't determine how to help someone feel included without each employee identifying how they are diverse and what they need. Each employee's internal biases may be blinding them to how they are perceived. The following recommendations should help to assist with both issues.

## Assign a Champion (or Multiple)

As discussed, there are many demographics that could play a role in diversity and inclusion. Rather than trying to decide how every diverse group wants to be heard, look for multiple champions to lead the effort. They can drive conversations with those they work with and share knowledge about how to address inclusion for what makes them diverse. Note that this isn't one solution for all. As an example, some deaf employees may prefer to only communicate via text. Others may prefer to use an ASL interpreter to communicate. Still others may prefer to lip-read. Likewise, a neurodivergent individual may require alone time without distraction to get work done. They may also not respond in chats or emails immediately.

## Create an Accountability Matrix to Hold Others Accountable

While assigning champions can be a big start, it is not the only step. There must be an accountability matrix. For example, your champions might be responsible for holding lunch and learns once a quarter. However, they should not be the only people responsible for inclusivity. Working group management and employees need to make inclusivity a priority. Adding diversity and inclusion training/participation key performance indicators (KPIs) to each role will assist with that.

## Address Harassment & Bullying Before It Happens

HR addresses harassment and bullying at a corporate level, but it is important that it becomes more than that. Colleagues often click through required training without truly absorbing the information. Then they are surprised when another colleague feels harassed or bullied. People tend to notice when others are wrong, but they are unable to see that they are also wrong. They don't see how they are playing a part in the issue. For example, one might see that someone else is acting passive-aggressive toward another colleague. That person might decide to keep quiet because they feel it isn't their business. Likewise, someone could be the passive-aggressive colleague unknowingly and be causing unknown harm. Of course there is always the possibility that this isn't the case and they are fully aware of their actions.

There is no excuse. Harassment and bullying are not acceptable behaviors. They damage the team's productivity in many ways. Everyone must take a stand to remove harassment and bullying from the workplace. This is especially important for management at the team level.

Ideas to improve team knowledge:

- Bring up the topic in team meetings.
- Invite guest speakers to speak and increase awareness.
- Review the training that HR provided as a team.
- Communicate regularly with your teams about how they can bring up concerns in an in-person or anonymous format.
- Hold discussion groups during lunch hours.
- Ask your team for ideas.
- Build diversity and inclusion concepts into team member KPIs on their quarterly review (see performance goals and objectives below for more information on how to do this) like:
  - Attended diversity and inclusion training.
  - Attended harassment and bullying table talk.
  - Led a discussion group on a topic regarding diversity and inclusion.

## Hiring and Recruiting

### Gaps in the Process

Consider the gaps between the DEI initiatives of your organization, the hiring practices of your department, and the recruiting practices for openings in your department hiring specifically. Are all three aligned to ensure you get diverse candidates? Unclear objectives will result in lost opportunities.

Root cause analysis can be very helpful here. Root cause analysis is often used in our day-to-day lives to address the core issues. We often forget that we can use those principles to improve other company practices as well. For example, the values/principles model (VPM) can be used to address the gap. The model is based on four values: representation, participation, application, and appreciation. The VPM provides a structured and measurable framework for transforming the workplace while hiring or recruiting.

**Representation**

Representation is rooted in the idea that diversity is an asset. When we recognize people for their individuality and unique voice, our experiences become richer and more profoundly human. Meaningful representation requires that marginalized people not be included merely for appearances or to fill a quota. Rather, organizations must remove barriers to demographic representation while also embracing individuals' unique skills, backgrounds, and contributions. When an organization includes people with diverse sociocultural, educational, and economic backgrounds and experiences, it signals that many types of people can succeed there. Representation doesn't just empower those who have been denied a presence—it encourages us to learn about and learn from people who are unlike us.

- Identify key open positions/departments now and in the future that could be targeted for growth in DEI
    - The key positions should include senior leaders, middle managers, and rank-and-file employees
- Survey your existing hiring managers
- Evaluate your job postings and descriptions:
    - Are you limiting potential candidates because the job posting is restrictive or focused on a limited demographic?
    - Are you limiting potential candidates because the job posting indicates a required degree or desired education at a specific school?

- Evaluate interviewing process and questions with your HR department to ensure you are exploring questions about how the candidate will bring new and diverse ideas or practices to your group.
    - Focus should be on what they bring to the department, not necessarily how they fit culturally
        - Will they push the team to be better?
        - Do they have the knowledge they need to raise the bar of the whole team?
        - Will they bring processes into the team that didn't exist before?
    - Are you blocking certain demographics because you aren't inclusive in that process? Ideas include:
        - Consider (dis)abilities or cognitive differences
            - Are you asking the candidates if they need accommodations and, if so, which ones?
            - Are you considering their communication style and is the process welcoming?
    - Where are you posting open positions? Is it a place where you would reach a different demographic or are you limiting it to schools and universities that have experienced employees?

- Determine a communication plan for hiring managers
  - Cultural change requires us all to work together and a proper communication plan will help to make that happen
- Modify plan over time

### Adopt Entrepreneurial Leadership

Managers and front-line employees need to become engaged in problem-solving to achieve the four values. To empower employees, organizations need to bring more visibility to the diversity within. One way to do so is to cross-train managers and rotate them through departments. That way they will be exposed to different aspects of the organization and to diverse people. These experiences help advance DEI in several ways. Managers will develop empathy for people with different skills, backgrounds, and experiences as they encounter them across the organization. They can also uncover pockets of untapped expertise and gain an understanding of the challenges or obstacles employees may face. With this knowledge about how different people operate and what they need to succeed, managers can take more initiative. They can clear a path for employees whose achievements may not have been previously visible or who need support to develop their talents. They can decide to fill a role with someone who lacks traditional credentials but who has demonstrated the necessary skills and aptitude.

### Modify the Plan Over Time: Apply the Application Techniques

These systems include how organizations develop and promote employees, define job titles, and even create and sell products. Changing them is difficult because it's hard for organizations to change how they do anything. Even leaders may fail to understand how their organization's processes may exclude people. Some members of the organization may resist changing existing processes if they benefit. Successful application should also be evident in an organization's products and services. Products designed for the average customer won't meet the needs of many. Organizations that adopt inclusive design learn to see that no customer is average. As a result, they learn to serve their customers better.

## Engage the Community

### Identify Community Partners

Identifying community partners to join you in your diversity and inclusion endeavor will have multiple positive outcomes. While some of these community partners will be able to train your team on local demographics and issues, others will be able to partner with you to educate and train potential employees. Still others will be able to talk to the schools about the opportunities nearby, what they look like and how to improve interest among the student population. You could even identify community partners that allow your employees to volunteer to build an open and inclusive environment between your corporation and your local community. All these strategies can assist in improving diversity and inclusion within your team members.

### Identify Training Opportunities

Have you considered that the local high school or community college students in your area may benefit from a partnership with you? As identified in the statistics section, our industry is facing a worker shortfall we are not ready for. By partnering with your local high schools, community colleges, or after school clubs, you can increase access to the labor pool. Sharing job opportunities with these groups might inspire students to pursue a relevant education. After their education, they might apply to your company, ready to get started.

After identifying the employee shortage, 3M has actively pursued this approach in the areas surrounding their factories. The results have been positive. For more information, visit the 3M website and check out the social aspect of their global impact.

Another demographic to consider is the demographic of disabled people who are looking for work. Accenture recently came out with an interesting report called *Getting to Equal: The Disability Inclusion Advantage | Accenture*[4]. It is a great resource for those looking to include disability as one of their diversity and inclusion campaigns.

This quote sheds some light on the importance of disability inclusion:

> "Persons with disabilities present business and industry with unique opportunities in labor force diversity and corporate culture, and they're a large consumer market eager to know which businesses authentically support their goals and dreams. Leading companies are accelerating disability inclusion as the next frontier of corporate social responsibility and mission-driven investing."
> -Ted Kennedy, Jr.

## Engage your Current Employees

### Annual and Quarterly Goals

Earlier in this report, we introduced quarterly KPIs as a way of reducing bullying or harassment. That strategy applies here, too. One of the most effective ways to ensure that a diversity and inclusion program is successful is to set performance goals for all employees at all levels of engagement. If done well, change comes from within and drives the right results. Consider aligning these goals not only to diversity and inclusion initiatives, but also to improving teamwork interdepartmentally. That way overall company results are improved. When all departments are aligned on goals, they can work as one organism toward the same goals and objectives.

It is important to consider the goals based on position and ability to follow through. For example, it's not appropriate to assign a goal to "create an employee resource group (ERG)" to someone who is on the front lines, working day-to-day next to equipment and with multiple departments. Instead, consider performance goals that speak to how an inclusive employee would work in their day-to-day. Maybe it might be to participate in an ERG activity of your choosing each quarter. It could also be to reach out to colleagues in other departments prior to scheduling maintenance to ensure they are aware and don't have a conflict. Both allow the employee to grow and increase their awareness of how their work affects others.

At the manager level, similar goals should be assigned that hold them accountable. Examples might include: "ensure employees are given time in their day to attend an ERG" or "connect employees with other departments that are affected by their work."

Again, the level of performance goal and the timing should be aligned. One shouldn't identify a goal of "attend an ERG activity of your choosing" if an ERG does not exist. These goals should be considered from the perspective of your company and what you currently have, as well as what your employees need to feel like they belong.

It is important to note: to do this appropriately, reach out to the human resources or people and culture department in your organization. Know that they will be your allies in this endeavor, as they have been wanting this kind of engagement for quite a while and are likely already aware of the need.

One final note on this subject:

While this may seem like this is something that should be addressed from top-down—much higher than your pay grade—it is imperative that people from reliability and asset management take ownership of the goals and objectives within your own departments. Even if this would normally be someone else's responsibility, act within your own department. Only you and your teams can address diversity and inclusion from within the walls of the organization. Address and change the day-to-day actions of your team members.

**Surveys**

Surveys are a great way to understand where you are at and where you want to be. They can show results and can give you an return on investment (ROI) on how DEI initiatives have impacted reliability. Consider what data you would like to be able to track over time. Also note that changing the wording or questions in the surveys will potentially give you different results. It is important to consider the goals of the survey and the data that will be needed to address those goals. Keep in mind that some of the data may already be available via human resources and a survey may not be needed.

Surveys are a great way to understand your employees, but surveys only work if the data is secure and input is protected. This means more than simply addressing their concerns with a statement. Being transparent with the data while protecting anonymity is paramount. If you get results from your survey that show there is work to be done, be open about that and then ask for honest feedback on how to address it. Honor their input in these voluntary surveys and let them know their honesty is appreciated.

Consider only asking for data that is needed. Your first thought may be to track the aspects that may make each employee diverse and then evaluate whether they feel as though they belong. That means you, as an employer, potentially have information that could make someone else vulnerable or open you up to liability. Therefore, focus on the results of the questions—not what makes each person unique.

Rather than try to recreate something that has already been done multiple times before, we have chosen to provide a few resources below that will assist you in developing your survey. The number of questions and their wording vary, but the intent is very similar. Below are some examples:

1. Diversityintech.co has a great article about the Top 20 survey questions for measuring inclusion at work. While this is not a complete list of possible questions, it's a fantastic place to start. It even considers whether the question should be an open-ended question or limited in response. If you just started with this, you would already have a great understanding of how your colleagues are feeling now and where you need to go.

2. There is a free template from Poppulo.com called *How to Measure Belonging in Your Workforce*. It provides 23 survey questions and evaluates how you are doing in three areas. However, it does require you to enter your contact information prior to downloading. If you don't want to do this, go with the first option. One important note about this template: It does give some great best practices and examples of how to set up the survey to get the best possible results, which is why we chose to share it here.

3. If you already use SurveyMonkey® for other surveys, this can be a great tool to utilize. Developed with Paradigm, the SurveyMonkey® template for diversity and inclusion will allow you to learn how your employees feel about their work environment. This template also seeks to understand the extent to which they feel they can truly thrive at your company. If you don't want to have to worry about how to gather the data or have to create the survey in another system, this might be the easy option for you.

**Personality and Communication Styles and Coaching**

In a recent presentation at the International Maintenance Conference in 2022, Melissa Ruth discussed how personality and communication styles affect how people respond to our leadership. Just like understanding learning styles helps us to create training that is more affective, so does understanding how people hear us and process what we have to say. The human mind and heart are complex, so it is important to note that understanding these specifics is only part of the battle here. This is made even more complex by adding to it neurodivergence and diversity of thought. So, how does one go about beginning to understand how to communicate effectively and get the results they need?

Take a moment here to think about each of your team members and their managers. Have you ever had an employee who didn't work well with another employee or a manager who failed to get results? We tend to believe that the person in your mind is not meant to be in that team or maybe even be a manager. We naturally assume they just weren't made for maintenance and reliability.

What if, instead, we gave them each the ability to understand how personalities and communication styles affected their results? This requires understanding both the way they communicate and the way their communication is interpreted.

There are many ways to understand this that don't require a degree in neuroscience. Additionally, many personality tools can be used here. Among them (in no particular order) are DiSC®, Enneagram, Personality Plus (now called "Wired That Way"), Myers-Briggs Type Indicator®, CliftonStrengths, 16 Personalities, 4 Color Personality Test, etc. There are so many assessments that it can be overwhelming to decide on which one. The truth is, they all bring value to the table. They all break down how your employee communicates naturally and how to adjust their communication style based on who they are talking with.

Taking these personality assessments is not only about the individual employee—it's about the team. Consider for a moment what a team might look like if they all had the same personality type and, therefore, all communicated the same way. Is this team one that everyone else wants to work with? Do people groan inwardly when you tell them they must work with them? Ouch. This is a perfect example of diversity and inclusion. It helps us to see the value of bringing in others who think and communicate differently from us.

It doesn't end with your evaluation of the team. It requires a few more things to consider:

1. Bring these learnings outside of the initial training and assessment process. How many times have you attended a training, learned a lot, but then failed to apply it afterward? If you want to get the most out of this endeavor, it cannot just be about the initial experience. Consider actionable events that will move the lessons from the theory to application. Make the information relevant. Push the personality test information further into the workplace. Use visual markers to communicate personality assessment results through the company. Some examples are:

    a. Using the True Colors assessment results as a guide, the organization provides each employee with Lego® bricks (as shown below) in the four colors. Employees would place bricks on their desks in the order of communication style that was important to them. This gives other team members a quick visual reminder of that person's communication preferences.

b. The organization first ensures each employee takes the CliftonStrengths assessment as part of their onboarding process. Afterwards, each employee is given training on how to build on their top five strengths. They were then provided color-coded PowerPoint® backgrounds with the ability to enter their unique strengths in the upper right corner. Then, they make it a background for online meeting platforms to communicate to other employees when on virtual meetings.

c. Using another type of assessment based on the True Colors test, the organization provided stickers. Employees put them on their badges and on doors to allow people to understand as they spoke to each other (or before they walked into the room) what their dominant type was. Coworkers would then be able to modify their communication styles appropriately.

2. Remember that you will be bringing in new employees in the future, so you will need to have a plan to keep the process going. Otherwise, this process has the potential of negatively affecting the culture because the new employees will not understand the meaning of terminology used by the existing employees who have been through the training.

3. While it's great for each employee to understand their personality styles and those of their teammates, don't lose sight of the value there is for management to understand their personality types. A department went through the personality styles assessment and found that their entire team was one personality style. All members were the type A personality. Management had to determine what they were missing and how to balance that personality style. They began balancing the team by partnering members with people from another department who had different personalities. This exercise had a few benefits. By assessing each employee and understanding how they entered the room, they were aware that some customers would fail to appreciate that personality. It also allowed for a new perspective to enter the team. Those that were more analytical and methodical were able to provide a value they hadn't before in the team. Lastly, they were able to understand why previous analytically-oriented training had failed to be effective in that team. It was because these team members were not thinkers—they were doers. They were able to change the method of training to ensure they got the right information at the right time, in the right way. In conclusion, they got better results.

4. Once you have completed these steps, ensure that your communication plans align to all personality and communication styles involved. Consider that some people will respond well to being directly ordered, while others will respond negatively. You will be amazed at the results when you do this. ■

# Putting It All Together

Now that you have read the sections, it is time to consider which suggested actions to add to your personal action plans moving forward. There are many actionable ideas shared in this document, but it cannot stop there.

We have discussed reasons to care about diversity, equity, inclusion and belonging (DEIB), the state of the workforce, barriers to DEIB and how to overcome them, ways to address your hiring practices and, finally, ways to engage your own employees. Yet, none of this information matters if you don't choose to put any of it into action.

Therefore, as we wrap things up here, we want to challenge you to develop a plan and then put it into action. Consider your employees as more than just assets to bring your company reliability. Rather, consider them as advocates who can make the company better than it was before.

❶ What three aspects will you put into action now?

❷ Which one or two will you share with someone else?

❸ Who will you work with to make things happen?

**KEEP IN MIND:** To fully embrace inclusion and belonging, one must consider that it's not just about your team—it's about the entire company ensuring facility reliability. This also means embracing the idea that outside viewpoints increase reliability and are critical to your success. ■

## Remember: Reliability is everyone's responsibility ...but do they know it?

---

### References:

1. **An Introduction to the Implicit Association Test** (IAT) – https://youtu.be/Hp8QK7TUxjc
2. **Project Implicit** - https://www.projectimplicit.net/
3. **The Harvard Implicit Association Test** - https://www.bing.com/ck/a?!&&p=dcde107ed79ff603JmltdHM9MTY2MTEzMTU3OCZpZ3VpZD0zN2Q0Yzg1OS1hMzYzLTQxNzItOTI3OS1iNmIzODNiYzVjOTgmaW5zaWQ9NTQyOQ&ptn=3&hsh=3&fclid=6baf5a07-21b9-11ed-90cd-d13b93f0dd5c&u=a1aHR0cHM6Ly9pbXBsaWNpdC5oYXJ2YXJkLmVkdS9pbXBsaWNpdC90YWtlYXRlc3QuaHRtbA&ntb=1
4. **Getting to Equal: The Disability Inclusion Advantage | Accenture.** https://www.accenture.com/t20181108t081959z__w__/us-en/_acnmedia/pdf-89/accenture-disability-inclusion-research-report.pdf

# Connecting Leaders to Evolve Asset Management

## Our AIM

To create a safe space for professional women to explore inquires around personal, professional, financial and organizational performance related to sustainability, reliability and asset management.

## Join WIRAM

- Professional peer group
- Opportunities for local group leadership
- Learn leadership skills and traits
- Expand your network
- Publish trought leadership papers
- Monthly networking webinars

## Advocates

## Visit Us!
www.AssetManagementProfessionals.org